# SURINAME
## in Pictures

**VGS**

Tom Streissguth

**TF CB**
**Twenty-First Century Books**

# Contents

Lerner Publishing Group, Inc. realizes that current information and statistics quickly become out of date. To extend the usefulness of the Visual Geography Series, we developed www.vgsbooks.com, a website offering links to up-to-date information, as well as in-depth material, on a wide variety of subjects. All of the websites listed on www.vgsbooks.com have been carefully selected by researchers at Lerner Publishing Group, Inc. However, Lerner Publishing Group, Inc. is not responsible for the accuracy or suitability of the material on any website other than www.lernerbooks.com. It is recommended that students using the Internet be supervised by a parent or teacher. Links on www.vgsbooks.com will be regularly reviewed and updated as needed.

Website address: www.lernerbooks.com

Twenty-First Century Books
A division of Lerner Publishing Group, Inc.
241 First Avenue North
Minneapolis, MN 55401 U.S.A.

Library of Congress Cataloging-in-Publication Data

Streissguth, Thomas, 1958–
      Suriname in pictures / by Tom Streissguth.
         p.   cm. — (Visual geography series)
      Includes bibliographical references and index.
      ISBN 978-1-57505-964-8 (lib. bdg. : alk. paper)
      1. Suriname—Juvenile literature. I. Title.
   F2408.5.S77 2010
   988.3—dc22                              2008050110

Manufactured in the United States of America
1 2 3 4 5 6 – BP – 15 14 13 12 11 10

# INTRODUCTION

Suriname is a small, sparsely settled nation on the northeastern coast of South America. Most of Suriname's people live in the north, near the Atlantic Ocean. In the south, scattered villages dot the dense tropical rain forest. A few roads and airstrips link these villages.

Suriname and two of its neighbors, Guyana and French Guiana, form a South American region called Guiana. For thousands of years, this region was home to peoples such as the Caribs, the Arawaks, and the Surinen. They survived by hunting animals, gathering wild foods, farming, and fishing. The Caribs and Arawaks built settlements throughout the Caribbean basin (the lands around and the islands in the Caribbean Sea).

Farmers from Britain and the Netherlands began arriving in Guiana in the 1600s. They established plantations (large farms for growing cash crops, such as sugarcane) along the coast. But the dense inland forests—and the native peoples who lived there—discouraged settlement of the interior. In addition, fertile soil and valuable minerals such as silver and gold seemed to be scarce inland.

Britain and the Netherlands fought over Guiana throughout the 1600s and 1700s. For short periods, Britain ruled the Dutch settlers from the Netherlands. But in 1674, Suriname officially became a Dutch colony, or dependent territory. Britain finally gave up its claim in 1815. Suriname was called Dutch Guiana during colonial times.

Colonial plantations grew crops such as cotton, cacao (the source of chocolate), rice, and sugarcane. To work the plantations, settlers imported slaves from Africa. Many slaves escaped and formed villages in the interior. These people became known as Maroons. Slavery continued in Dutch Guiana until the late 1800s.

After slavery ended, the colony still needed laborers. So through the early 1900s, it hired workers from another Dutch colony, the Netherlands Indies (modern Indonesia), and from India and China. Many of these workers stayed. As a result, Dutch Guiana became a land of diverse ethnic groups, cultures, and religions.

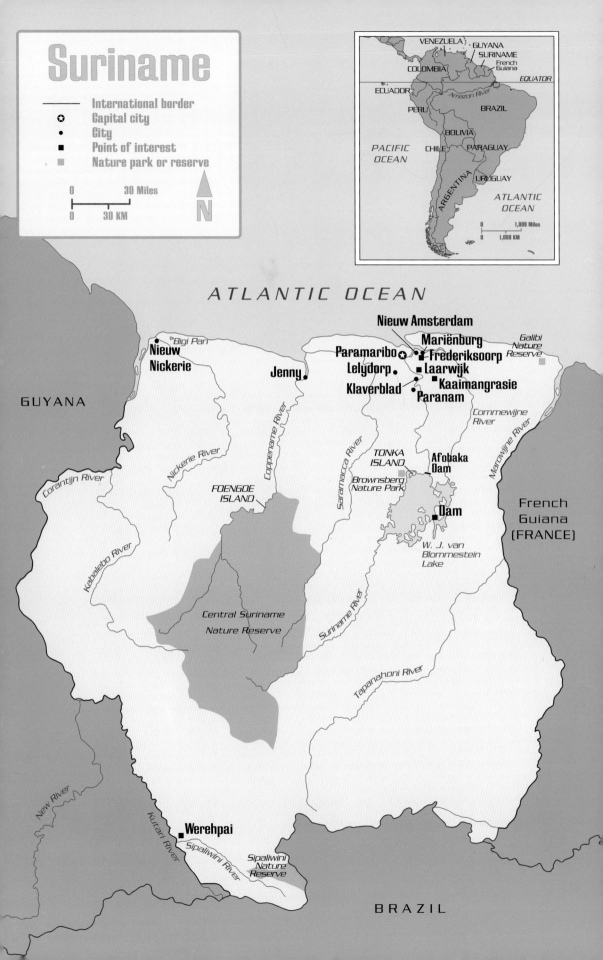

Suriname gained independence in 1975. Soon afterward, a group of military leaders overthrew the civilian (nonmilitary) government. The new leaders squashed free speech and jailed their opponents. In the 1980s, rebel groups in the south mounted a violent uprising that lasted several years.

In the 1990s, Suriname returned to civilian government. In addition, rebel and government forces signed a peace agreement and stopped fighting.

Yet Suriname still faced social and economic troubles. In the early twenty-first century, Surinamese workers staged frequent strikes (work stoppages) to protest low wages and high prices. Many Surinamese struggled with unemployment, limited education and health care, and poor living conditions. The government had trouble balancing its budget and paying its debts to foreign nations.

The economy of modern Suriname depends heavily on farming and the mining of bauxite (aluminum ore). Tourism holds promise as a new source of jobs and income. But Suriname needs foreign investment to make use of its many natural resources, such as timber, hydroelectricity, minerals, and oil. Suriname also needs careful planning to develop its economy in a way that won't damage the environment—and the promise of tourism.

Suriname is home to several political parties, which formed in the mid-1900s around independence leaders. Each party represents the interests of one ethnic group. No party holds a majority of seats in Suriname's government, so the parties form coalitions (partnerships) to achieve their goals.

Suriname's ethnic groups have lived side by side fairly peacefully throughout the country's modern history. And the political parties give a voice to each group among the country's five hundred thousand people. Yet the parties and coalitions often disagree on the best way forward. The result is uncertainty over Suriname's future economic and social policies.

Visit www.vgsbooks.com for links to websites with additional information about the land, history, government, people, culture, and economy of Suriname.

# THE LAND

Suriname is a small country in northeastern South America. Its neighbors are Guyana to the west, French Guiana to the east, and Brazil to the south. The northern coast faces the Atlantic Ocean. The smallest country in South America, Suriname has an area of 63,039 square miles (163,270 square kilometers). It is a bit smaller than the U.S. state of Wisconsin.

## Topography

Four main land zones make up Suriname. These are the coastal plain, the northern savanna (grassland), the highlands, and the Sipaliwini Savanna.

A narrow plain follows the entire Atlantic coast, which is about 240 miles (386 km) long. This plain stretches about 10 miles (16 km) inland. The plain is slightly wider in the west than in the east. This is Suriname's most densely populated region.

The coastal terrain is low and flat. Rivers empty into the ocean all along the shore, creating a series of estuaries. (Estuaries are bodies of water in which fresh river water mixes with salty seawater.) This

region has few natural sand beaches. Marshes and mangroves line the seacoast. (Mangroves are shrubs and small trees that flourish in salty water.) Wilderness areas separate the towns and ports. In some places, dikes and holding ponds prevent flooding from the sea.

South of the coastal plain lies a wider and higher plain. This zone, called the northern savanna, is actually a patchwork of savanna and forest. The region is about 40 miles (64 km) wide. It contains many bauxite deposits and mines. Narrow roads link the scattered mines, towns, and plantations.

Farther south, the plain rises gradually to steep hills. The hills and mountains of southern Suriname are part of the Guiana Highlands. This mountain range stretches from eastern Venezuela across Guyana, Suriname, French Guiana, and northern Brazil.

Suriname's highlands consist of four distinct mountainous areas. From west to east are the Bakhuis Mountains, the Wilhelmina Mountains, the Van Asch van Wijk Mountains, and the Tumuc-Humac

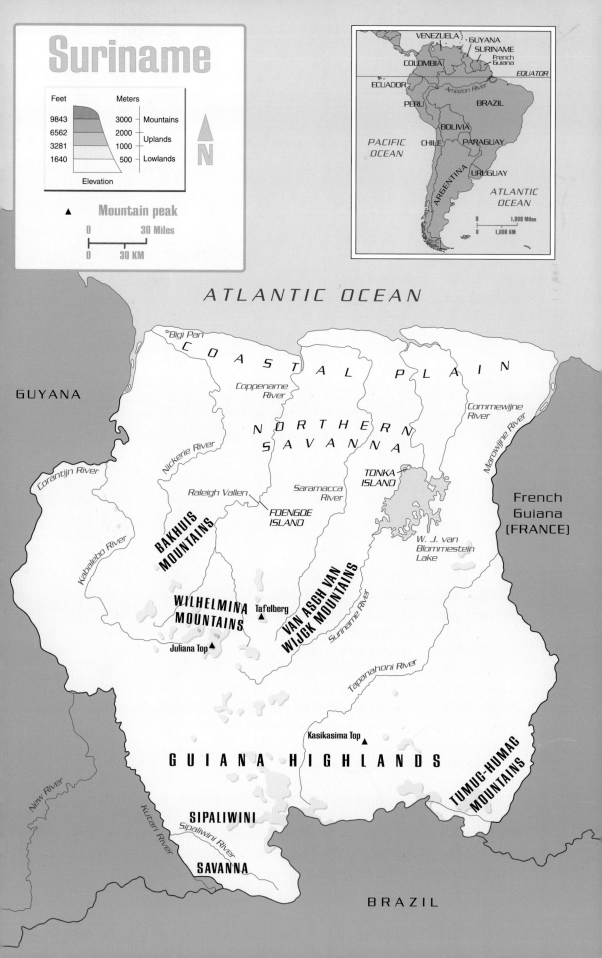

# Suriname

VENEZUELA · GUYANA
SURINAME
French
Guiana
COLOMBIA
EQUATOR
ECUADOR
PERU
BRAZIL
BOLIVIA
CHILE
PARAGUAY
PACIFIC
OCEAN
ARGENTINA
URUGUAY
ATLANTIC
OCEAN

0          1,000 Miles
0          1,000 KM

ATLANTIC OCEAN

GUYANA

French
Guiana
[FRANCE]

Bigi Pan

C O A S T A L   P L A I N

Coppename
River

Commewijne
River

Corantijn River

Nickerie River

N O R T H E R N
S A V A N N A

TONKA
ISLAND

Marowijne River

Raleigh Vallen

Saramacca
River

Kabalebo River

BAKHUIS
MOUNTAINS

FOENGOE
ISLAND

W. J. van
Blommestein
Lake

WILHELMINA
MOUNTAINS

Tafelberg ▲

VAN ASCH VAN
WIJCK MOUNTAINS

Juliana Top ▲

Suriname River

Tapanahoni River

New River

Kasikasima Top ▲

G U I A N A   H I G H L A N D S

TUMUC-HUMAC
MOUNTAINS

Kutari River

SIPALIWINI

Sipaliwini River

SAVANNA

BRAZIL

Mountains. Juliana Top, the highest point in Suriname at 4,035 feet (1,230 meters), lies in the Wilhelmina Mountains.

Dense rain forest covers Suriname's highlands. Isolated Arawak, Carib, and Maroon villages nestle in small clearings. The region has few roads. Many places are accessible only by small aircraft. Some parts of this forest are uninhabited and unexplored.

In southernmost Suriname is the Sipaliwini Savanna. This region borders the winding Sipaliwini River. The grassland includes small islands of rain forest and palm groves. It is uninhabited, except for small groups of nomads, who move their home base according to the season.

## Rivers and Lakes

### TWO COUNTRIES, TWO BORDERS

Suriname and Guyana have been arguing over their southern border for many years. The Surinamese believe the border runs along the New River, a tributary of the Corantijn. The Guyanese believe the border follows the Kutari River, another Corantijn tributary east of the New River. The two nations have also disputed their maritime border. The United Nations (an international diplomatic organization) finally settled the maritime dispute in 2007. But Guyana and Suriname are still disputing their southern border.

Suriname's rivers rise in the highlands and generally flow northward into the sea. Many serve as important transportation routes. Artificial channels link the rivers, allowing boat transport over long distances.

The rivers carry silt, or fine soil, downstream to the coast. As they approach the ocean, they split into several branches and form wide deltas. The river deltas give way to estuaries. Along the coast, the estuaries open into a series of wide bays.

The Corantijn River forms the Guyana-Suriname border. Its source lies in northern Brazil. One of its main tributaries (feeder rivers) is the Kabalebo River, which begins in the Wilhelmina Mountains. The Kabalebo draws tourists who enjoy fishing and bird-watching along its banks. The Corantijn River ends in a long, wide mouth at the city of Nieuw Nickerie.

The Nickerie River begins in the Bakhuis Mountains and flows through northwestern Suriname. This waterway feeds Bigi Pan, a vast wetland near the ocean. Many varieties of fish and shellfish thrive in the tidal mudflats, creeks, mangroves, forests, swamps, and lagoons of Bigi Pan. Small-scale commercial fishing is an important part of the area's economy. The Nickerie River empties into the Atlantic Ocean at Nieuw Nickerie.

Suriname's river deltas have played an important role in the national economy. Throughout the coastal region, Dutch colonists and African slaves built polders, rectangular areas of raised earth surrounded by ditches. The polders created cropland safe from high tides and river flooding.

The Coppename River rises in the Wilhelmina Mountains. It flows northward through a series of rapids and waterfalls. Hills and dense forest hem in this river. During colonial times, many escaped slaves settled along its banks. The Saramacca River, which begins in the Van Asch van Wijk Mountains, joins the Coppename River near the seacoast town of Jenny.

The Suriname River begins in the Wilhelmina Mountains and flows through northeastern Suriname. In the middle of its course, the Afobaka Dam creates the W. J. van Blommestein Lake. This lake is the largest body of water in Suriname. The dam harnesses the power of rushing water to generate hydroelectricity. Bauxite processing plants in the area rely on this source of energy. The Suriname River continues northward through the capital city, Paramaribo. It empties into the sea just north of town.

The Marowijne River forms the Suriname–French Guiana border. The Tapanahoni River, a main tributary of the Marowijne, rises along the southern border and flows northeastward across central Suriname.

## ◉ Climate

Suriname lies just north of the equator, or the center belt of Earth. Its tropical climate means average temperatures stay high throughout the year. The country receives plentiful rainfall brought by ocean winds.

A long rainy season runs from March to August. As high winds and rain move southward toward the Amazon River (the largest and longest river in the Americas), a drier season begins. The dry season lasts from September to November. This season is the hottest time of year. A brief period of moderate rainfall and cooler temperatures occurs in December and January. Another short dry period follows in February and March.

Rainfall is heaviest in the central and southeastern mountains. Along the coast, rainfall decreases from west to east. In Paramaribo, average annual rainfall is 95 inches (241 centimeters). To the east, average rainfall drops to about 76 inches (193 cm) per year.

The capital is warm and humid throughout the year, but constant sea breezes cool the city's residents. Temperatures reach about 86°F (30°C) during the day. Nights are typically a comfortable 72°F (22°C).

## Natural Resources

Suriname's interior is rich in timber and minerals that provide valuable exports. The country contains large deposits of bauxite, gold, nickel, copper, platinum, iron ore, and kaolin (a white clay used in ceramics).

The country also has sizable deposits of crude oil. Suriname harnesses the energy of fast-flowing rivers to generate hydroelectricity for its cities and industries.

The coast teems with shellfish, such as shrimp and crabs, which support a small fishing industry. The coastal river deltas also have fertile land and ample rainfall. These resources support a variety of cash crops, such as rice, bananas, coconut palms, and peanuts.

## Flora and Fauna

Coastal Suriname is home to abundant wildlife. Its cities are small, and the overall population is low. This allows animals to thrive in the wetlands along the shore. Birds such as white herons, egrets, scarlet ibises, and storks favor the mangroves. Four kinds of sea turtles nest on the Matapica beach northeast of Paramaribo. The coastal region also hosts sea otters, caimans (a type of alligator), dolphins, and manatees (large aquatic mammals related to elephants).

**Giant river otters** live along the banks of Suriname's rivers. This endangered animal can grow to be up to 6 feet (1.8 m) long.

Suriname's rain forest shelters more than one hundred mammal species (kinds), including howler monkeys and tapirs (horselike animals with flexible snouts). Large wildcats such as jaguars, pumas, and ocelots are common in the Central Suriname Nature Reserve. The capybara, the world's largest rodent, also lives in the forest. Colorful parrots, macaws, toucans, and cocks-of-the-rock fly through the forest canopy, or upper layer.

**Poison dart frogs get their name from indigenous (native) hunters. Hunters extract poison from the frogs and dip their arrows and blowgun darts in it. The frogs' brilliant coloring warns predators not to eat them.**

Hundreds of different reptiles and amphibians live in Suriname. Its large, deadly snakes include boa constrictors, anacondas, and bushmasters. Poison dart frogs are plentiful. These frogs have brightly colored, toxic skin. Mata mata turtles (also called alligator snapping turtles) lurk in the rivers.

The Surinamese rain forest has a dense understory (a lower layer of vegetation). The understory gives way to a canopy full of palm fronds and tree branches. High above the canopy, emergent trees rise like giant umbrellas. Towering mahogany and kapok trees are common. These trees can reach heights of 130 feet (40 m). The flowering plants of Suriname include orchids, hibiscus, oleander, and bougainvillea.

Scientists working in Suriname's rain forest often discover unknown species. These new plants and animals may be useful for medicine and scientific research. The destruction of rain forest, however, poses a threat to further discoveries in Suriname.

## Environmental Issues

Rain forests cover more than half of Suriname, but they are slowly disappearing. The government rents public land to foreign companies that harvest timber. These companies typically practice clear-cutting. Logging in this way fells most or all of the trees in a harvest area.

Clear-cutting severely damages the environment. The practice destroys wildlife habitat and leads to soil erosion (washing away). It also dumps large amounts of carbon dioxide gas into the air, which worsens global climate change. To protect its remaining forests, Suriname has set up more than a dozen protected areas. In these areas, the government strictly limits—or forbids—logging, hunting, and farming.

Rice farming near the seacoast strongly affects the environment. Chemicals that protect rice seedlings from insects make their way into groundwater, posing danger to animals and humans. Irrigation systems

**Clear-cutting** destroyed this patch of rain forest in Suriname.

for watering crops take freshwater from streams and rivers. As a result, the wetlands receive less freshwater from the rivers and become too salty. Polders and dikes worsen this problem. Many marshes along the coast are growing so salty that some fish and waterfowl avoid them. The government is improving freshwater irrigation systems to solve this problem.

Urban pollution affects Paramaribo and other cities. Waterways flowing through these areas serve as sewers for trash, street runoff, and factory wastes. By improving sanitation (sewage and garbage collection), the city may be able to clean up its streets and waterways.

Another danger to groundwater is bauxite mining. Mines and processing plants often dump waste ore and harmful chemicals into streams. Mining operations also add to deforestation (clearing of trees). Suriname's government is trying to balance economic development with environmental preservation. It has forbidden mining in several protected areas. It enforces rules against hunting and clearing on public lands leased to mining companies.

Several species of animals in Suriname are endangered. These include the peregrine falcon, the leatherback turtle, the caiman, and the manatee.

## Cities

PARAMARIBO (population 250,000) is the capital of Suriname. It is one of the smallest national capitals in the world. The city lies on the Suriname River about 10 miles (16 km) from the Atlantic Ocean. Most Surinamese shorten the city's name to Parbo.

Dutch traders founded the city in the early 1600s. Fearing pirate raids, they built Paramaribo a safe distance from the seacoast. The Dutch colonists built canals and homes similar to those in the Netherlands.

The British captured the city in 1650 and made it the capital of a British colony. They raised Fort Willoughby to defend their claim. The fort fell to the Dutch in 1667. They renamed it Fort Zeelandia. The British and Dutch continued to fight over trade and navigation rights. The city suffered frequent raids until the British finally gave up all claims in Dutch Guiana in 1815.

Paramaribo became the capital of independent Suriname in 1975. It is the largest seaport in the country. The nation exports aluminum, timber, rice, bananas, and citrus fruits through this port. Factories in the city process timber, bauxite, food, beverages, and tobacco.

Paramaribo has a varied ethnic mix. Europeans originally settled the city. People from India, China, and Indonesia followed. Many indigenous people call the city home. Paramaribo also has a large Creole population. Creoles are descendants of African slaves and Europeans.

Independence Square forms the heart of the city. The Presidential Palace and the National Assembly building border the square. Many colonial buildings and canals survive in the modern city. In older neighborhoods, white clapboard houses with steep roofs and green shutters line the streets. Hindu temples, Islamic mosques, and Christian churches add architectural variety. The spires of Saints Peter

The historic district of Paramaribo features traditional Dutch architecture.

and Paul Cathedral, one of the world's largest wooden buildings, tower above the neighboring streets. Visitors may inspect Fort Zeelandia, the Cupchiik Coliseum, and the Numismatic Museum. The museum's collection of Surinamese coins dates back to 1679.

LELYDORP (population 19,000) is the second-largest city in Suriname. It is the capital of the Wanica district just west of Paramaribo. The city was originally named Kofi Djompo in honor of an early Maroon rebel leader. The town later changed its name to honor Cornelis Lely, a famous Dutch engineer and governor of Dutch Guiana. Lelydorp is the center of an important mining district.

NIEUW NICKERIE (population 13,000) is the third-largest city in Suriname. It lies at the mouth of the Corantijn River, opposite the town of Corriverton, Guyana. A ferry carries passengers back and forth across the border. Farmers from the surrounding countryside bring rice, citrus fruit, bananas, and other products to the busy market in Nieuw Nickerie. Some farmers come in search of better-paid urban work.

Nieuw Nickerie has historically been an important immigration center. The town has also become a center for illegal trade in gold and other goods. This underground economy, the movement of people across the border, and disputed fishing rights in the area cause tension between Suriname and Guyana.

> Visit www.vgsbooks.com for links to websites with additional information about the geography of Suriname, including more facts about the country's cities and natural resources.

# HISTORY AND GOVERNMENT

Historians and archaeologists have been exploring Suriname for decades. Throughout the country, they have found scattered remains of ancient societies.

In the Sipaliwini Savanna, archaeologists have found prehistoric stone weapons. They have also dug up the remains of tool-making workshops. From this evidence, experts conclude that about ten thousand years ago, people in the savannas of southern Suriname hunted mastodons and mammoths. These large, elephantlike animals began dying out around that time and have since become extinct.

Hunter-gatherers moved from place to place in search of game and wild foods. Their descendants learned how to clear forested land by cutting trees and burning undergrowth. Historians believe this slash-and-burn method created much of modern Suriname's savanna.

People of this region were in contact with groups to the west, in modern Guyana and Venezuela. They also traveled via tributaries of the Río Negro (Black River) south to the Amazon River basin. They

fashioned red and white pottery called Saladoid ware. Potters decorated their work with human and animal figures.

At least two thousand years ago, ancient people made petroglyphs (pictures carved in rock) along the seacoast and in the Corantijn and Marowijne river valleys. They also built burial mounds.

Terraced hillsides show that these ancient people farmed the land in the river valleys. They traded stone tools with people of the coast. The coastal people, in turn, traded with Caribbean island people. For many centuries, people migrated between the southern Caribbean islands and the Guiana coast.

## Arawaks and Caribs

The Arawak people moved northward from the Amazon River basin into Suriname at least one thousand years ago. They spread along the seacoast and to the Caribbean islands. Arawaks lived in small villages led by caciques (chiefs). Villagers cleared and farmed the surrounding fields. They grew a starchy edible root called cassava and hunted wild animals. They moved frequently in search of game and fertile soil.

The Caribs followed the Arawaks into Guiana from the Amazon region and farther south. Like the Arawaks, the Caribs lived on wild game and cassava. They were skilled warriors, boatbuilders, and navigators. They mined silver from deposits throughout northern South America and traded with the Taino people of the eastern Caribbean. The Caribs often warred with their rivals and raided Arawak villages.

Carib war parties spread fear throughout Guiana and the Caribbean. They eventually drove most of the Arawaks out of Suriname. A few independent Arawak villages survived. The Carib raiders took many Arawak captives. As a result of intermarriage, the two peoples blended in Suriname.

**The Surinen were an indigenous people of northern South America. The Caribs and the Arawaks drove the Surinen into the rain forests. By the 1500s, when Europeans arrived, the Surinen had disappeared. But their memory survives in the name of Suriname.**

Another people, the Surinen, lived near the coast. Like the Arawaks and the Caribs, they had migrated northward into Suriname. The Arawak and Carib peoples greatly outnumbered the Surinen. The Surinen were disappearing by the late 1400s. Eventually, their culture vanished, while small communities of Arawaks and Caribs survived.

## Europeans Arrive

In May 1498, Christopher Columbus began his third voyage to find a westward sea route from Europe to the Indian Ocean. Columbus sailed near the coast of Guiana in July. But he did not make landfall in this region. After Columbus, Spanish, Portuguese, French, British, and Dutch explorers visited Guiana throughout the 1500s.

Spain claimed the territory of Guiana in 1593. But few Spaniards ventured into the region to conquer land on Spain's behalf. Gold discoveries were few. And the marshy coast was ill suited for settlement.

Carib and Arawak villages remained along the coast and in the rain forest. Their residents attacked European landing parties and raided the small Spanish and English outposts. But the indigenous people were no match for European guns and swords. Foreign diseases also took a heavy toll. The Caribs and Arawaks soon disappeared from the coast. But small communities survived in the rain forest and savanna regions to the south.

A French explorer of the 1580s drew this picture of an **Arawak village.**

The first Dutch colonists came to Guiana in 1616. They explored the coast, looking for land suited to settlement. They built small towns and trading posts at the river mouths. The Dutch ventured inland only in search of game and freshwater.

In 1630 the British set up a small colony at Marshall's Creek, on the banks of the Suriname River. In 1650 a British group under Francis Willoughby and Laurens Hide captured the settlement at Paramaribo from the Dutch. This site lay farther inland along the Suriname River. British and Dutch farmers cleared land for plantations in northern Suriname. They grew coffee, cacao, sugarcane, and cotton for export to Europe.

In the meantime, other parts of Guiana were attracting European settlers too. The British were settling land to the west, in modern Guyana. Small French outposts were trading to the east, in modern French Guiana.

The Caribs sided with the British, while the Arawaks allied with the French and Dutch. The Dutch gathered Arawak raiding parties to attack their rivals. The Dutch also tried to set the Carib chiefs against each other and enlist Carib warriors to protect Dutch settlements.

## The Dutch Colony

In 1667 the Dutch and British signed the Treaty of Breda. By this agreement, the Dutch gave up New Amsterdam (modern Manhattan Island, a part of New York City). In exchange, the British gave up their claim to central Guiana, then being settled by the Dutch.

Most British settlers left Dutch Guiana. In the meantime, a new group of immigrants was arriving. They were Jews forced out of

Dutch and British representatives sign the **Treaty of Breda** in 1667.

colonial French Guiana and Brazil. Under David Nassy, their leader, they settled along the Suriname River.

## JEWS IN SURINAME

One of the first groups to settle in Suriname was a community of Jewish refugees. In the 1500s, many Portuguese and Spanish Jews fled to the Netherlands to escape religious persecution. When they encountered more trouble in the Netherlands, they sailed to South America. Many lived in areas of Dutch South America that later became part of colonial Brazil and French Guiana. In the mid-1600s, these Jews again fled religious intolerance and moved to Suriname. A small Jewish community still thrives in Paramaribo and other towns of modern Suriname.

Meanwhile, the Dutch and British kept wrangling over Dutch Guiana. In 1674 they signed the Treaty of Westminster, which officially made Suriname a Dutch colony.

The Dutch government granted the Dutch West India Company the right to administer the colony. This private company controlled Dutch Guiana's economy and settlement. The company's employees ventured inland to trade with Carib and Arawak villages. This trade often led to conflict. In exchange for banning certain troublesome traders, Carib chiefs let the Dutch build outposts in the interior.

In the late 1600s, few new settlers came from Europe. Dutch Guiana's natural resources were not easily accessible, and its fertile farmland was limited. In addition, the settlers suffered violent clashes with British pirates and indigenous people. The native people resisted European settlement of the interior. The Dutch brought in soldiers from Europe to guard against raids from hostile Caribs.

Dutch merchants neglected Guiana too. Dutch Guiana had limited value for the European market. The journey across the Atlantic and through the pirate-infested Caribbean was extremely dangerous. Dutch merchants focused on the Netherlands Indies. This vast colony in Southeast Asia had plentiful spices and hardwoods, which were very valuable in Europe.

In 1683, after the Dutch West India Company folded, the Dutch government named Cornelis van Aerssen van Sommelsdijk as the first governor of Dutch Guiana. Under his leadership, the colony began to thrive. New settlers built several hundred more small plantations along the coast to grow coffee, sugarcane, cotton, and cacao trees. The colonists built polders to protect their crops from flooding. To improve communications, Sommelsdijk ordered soldiers to dig a canal between the Suriname and Saramacca rivers.

But Sommelsdijk's stern leadership—and his use of soldiers as common laborers—earned him dangerous enemies. One of them murdered the governor in 1688.

## Maroon Revolt

To work their plantations, the Dutch colonists imported slaves from Africa. Several thousand slaves arrived in Dutch Guiana each year. Plantation owners bought slaves at a public market in Paramaribo.

Slavery in Suriname was a brutal institution. Slaves were mere property and had no legal rights. Their masters housed them in shacks and forced them to plant and harvest crops without pay. Slaveholders dealt out frequent beatings and whippings. They also put slaves to death for disobedience. Harsh treatment, disease, and hunger killed many slaves.

This brutality led to frequent clashes between slaves and slaveholders. Many slaves escaped. Runaway slaves fled upriver to remote areas of the rain forest, where they set up independent villages. Their descendants became known as Maroons. The Maroons formed distinct tribes, such as the Saramaccan, Boni, and Aukaner (also known as the Djuka).

Maroon raiding parties regularly attacked the Dutch plantations for food, weapons, and supplies. These raids continued for decades. Meanwhile, the colonists staged violent reprisals (revenge attacks).

Although sugarcane farming had begun to bring in large sums of money, Dutch Guiana struggled after Sommelsdijk's death. French pirates staged frequent raids on the coastal towns. In 1712 the French pirate Jacques Cassard came ashore with a large group. The pirates

## A Soldier Encounters Slavery

John Gabriel Stedman was born in 1744 to a Scottish father and a Dutch mother in the Netherlands. In the 1770s, he ventured to Dutch Guiana. As a Dutch soldier, he witnessed by slaveholders and military officers horrific abuse of the colony's slaves.

Stedman's memoir, *Narrative of a Five Years' Expedition against the Revolted Negroes of Surinam*, describes his experiences fighting against the colony's Maroons and rebellious slaves. The book became popular in Europe and prompted many to call for an end to slavery.

John Gabriel Stedman commissioned this **illustration of a hunt for escaped slaves** for his memoir.

wandered the countryside burning plantations, destroying crops, and demanding a large ransom (payment) to leave. The colonists paid the ransom, and Cassard's company left. Thousands of slaves escaped in the chaos.

Ongoing brutality prompted thousands more to escape slavery. The colony could not muster enough troops to deal with the growing—and ever more rebellious—Maroon population. Eventually, the Dutch reached a truce with the Maroons. Each year the colony would pay a sum of money or goods to the Maroon leaders. In return, the Maroons would cease their raids.

Throughout the 1700s, Dutch Guiana thrived. Rising sugar prices in Europe enriched the colony. Peace with the Maroons allowed the colony to prosper. Dutch Guiana became one of the Netherlands' most valuable colonies. At the same time, it became an inviting target for the British.

## International Troubles

In the late 1700s, British Guiana (the colony west of Dutch Guiana) became a source of trouble for the Dutch colonists. In 1780 British ships began raiding Dutch settlements in South America. British soldiers and adventurers captured the small Dutch colony of Demerara in western Dutch Guiana. This settlement became part of British Guiana.

British raids continued into the early 1800s. By this time, the British were also at war with a French army led by Napoleon Bonaparte. The Napoleonic Wars (1799–1815) were an effort by Bonaparte, the ruler of France, to control Europe.

The costs of this war prompted the British to sign a treaty called the Peace of Amiens in 1802. Among other things, this treaty required the British to surrender their claim to Dutch possessions in South America.

But this peace lasted only a year. The British retook Dutch Guiana in 1803. In 1815, after the final defeat of Bonaparte, the European nations signed the Treaty of Vienna. This agreement formally ended the Napoleonic Wars. The treaty also returned Dutch Guiana permanently to the Dutch.

While fighting in Europe, Britain had invested very little money or effort in Guiana. The colony had suffered as a result. By the time the Dutch regained Dutch Guiana, the Netherlands had turned its attention to the Netherlands Indies. Few merchants or settlers came to Dutch Guiana.

## Domestic Troubles

The 1800s were difficult for Dutch Guiana. Disasters worsened the economic slump caused by British and Dutch neglect. In 1821 and 1832, fires swept through Paramaribo. The blazes destroyed the city's rickety wooden buildings. In the 1850s, an outbreak of yellow fever (a deadly virus spread by mosquitoes) struck.

The end of slavery in Dutch Guiana complicated matters. For two centuries, Suriname's plantations had depended on slaves. But by the mid-1800s, an international antislavery movement was growing. British politicians led the way. They banned slavery in the British colonies in 1833, after the Napoleonic Wars ended. Dutch Guiana finally ended slavery in 1863. But the law banning slavery required freed slaves to do paid work on their plantations for ten years.

Meanwhile, the Dutch colonists demanded a body of elected representatives to look after the colony's affairs. The Netherlands still ruled Dutch Guiana through an appointed governor. The settlers had no representation in their government or power to pass their own laws.

In 1866 the Netherlands granted limited voting rights in Dutch Guiana. Male colonists paying taxes and holding property could elect nine members of a thirteen-member colonial assembly. The governor of the colony appointed the other four members.

In 1873 the freed slaves' ten years of required plantation work ended. Some joined the Maroons. Many former slaves moved to the cities. They made up a new majority of free citizens in Paramaribo and other towns. Citizens of African and European heritage became known as Creoles.

## Asian Laborers Arrive

Plantation owners in Dutch Guiana faced a sudden labor shortage in the 1870s. They arranged to have workers sail from India, China, and Java (an island in the Netherlands Indies). The workers agreed to stay for at least five years. After this period, they could continue working, move elsewhere within the colony, or return to their homelands.

The arrival of Indian, Javanese, and Chinese workers in the late 1800s and early 1900s transformed the society of Dutch Guiana. Europeans, Creoles, Maroons, indigenous peoples, and Asians all made important contributions to the colony. Different ethnic groups used different languages. They followed different religions. At the same time, shared interests—such as the desire for national autonomy and prosperity—began to evolve among the diverse peoples.

The plantation economy began failing in the early 1900s. Because landowners had to pay their workers, vast sugarcane, coffee, and cacao estates were no longer profitable. Many of the estates broke up into smaller farms. Others fell into disuse. Smaller farms began growing bananas, rice, and citrus fruits. A logging industry also developed in the forests of southern Suriname. The colony leased timber cutting and export rights to private companies from the United States and Europe.

Dutch Guiana's economy still relied on agriculture. Settlement remained sparse, and manufacturing was nearly nonexistent.

Some citizens began mining gold and searching for other valuable

### INDIANS ARRIVE

The first ship to bring Asian workers to Dutch Guiana arrived at Nieuw Amsterdam, a port across the river from Paramaribo, on June 5, 1873. The *Lalla Rookh* had been sailing for fourteen weeks from the port of Calcutta, India—a journey of more than 12,000 miles (19,300 km) in the days before the Panama Canal.

Aboard the ship were 399 contract laborers. They arrived exactly three weeks before the ten-year period of required labor for former slaves ended (July 1, 1873). The Indian workers were supposed to return home after five years, but most stayed. Indian workers also settled in British Guiana and the Caribbean island of Trinidad.

Irrigation ditches mark the edges of **abandoned plantation fields** in the countryside near Paramaribo.

minerals in the interior. Engineers built a short railway between Paramaribo and Dam, a settlement in the gold-mining region.

## The Bauxite Boom

The mining industry grew more important during World War I (1914–1918). In this war, the Central Powers and the Allied Powers fought each other in Europe. The United States joined the Allies in 1917. The Netherlands stayed neutral.

World War I raised the demand for aluminum, a light metal used in machinery, engines, and warplanes. People began exploring Dutch Guiana in search of bauxite, the raw ore used to make aluminum. The colony's first bauxite mines began operating in 1918.

By the 1920s, bauxite was an important export. Some factories in Dutch Guiana began refining the ore into aluminum. The Aluminum Company of America (ALCOA) bought mining rights and began operations in the colony.

In 1930 the Great Depression (a worldwide economic collapse, 1929–1939) hit Dutch Guiana. Trade slowed, aluminum factories shut down, and unemployment rose. Poverty spread throughout the colony. Economic problems inspired political protest among workers. A labor leader named Anton de Kom began calling for independence from the Netherlands.

In 1939 World War II (1939–1945) broke out in Europe. Germany invaded Poland, causing Britain and France to declare war on Germany. The war quickly spread throughout Europe and drew in many other nations too. Germany, Italy, Japan, and their allies (the Axis Powers)

A group of **Royal Dutch Marines** changes the guard at an outpost in Paramaribo in 1941.

fought on one side. On the other side fought a group called the Allied Powers, whose key members were Britain, the Soviet Union, the United States, and China.

Germany invaded and began occupying the Netherlands in 1940. This occupation—and the war at large—abruptly halted commerce between Europe and Dutch Guiana.

But Dutch Guiana was still mining bauxite and producing aluminum for export to the United States. When the United States entered World War II in 1941, demand for aluminum rose sharply. The United States used aluminum to make aircraft parts and other military equipment.

In 1945 the Axis Powers surrendered, and the war ended. After the war, many European colonies around the world began demanding independence. In response, the Netherlands allowed Dutch Guiana some self-rule.

## Independence

In the decade following World War II, several new political parties formed in Dutch Guiana. Each party appealed to a specific ethnic group. The Progressive Surinamese People's Party (PSP) and the Progressive National Party (PNP) represented the Creoles. The United Hindustani Party (VHP) stood for the interests of Indians. Javanese leaders formed the Indonesian Peasants Party (KTPI).

In 1948 Dutch Guiana held its first election for a colonial legislature. In 1954 the Netherlands made Dutch Guiana an autonomous territory. The territory was largely self-governing. The Netherlands kept control of Dutch Guiana's defense and foreign affairs.

The local leaders of Dutch Guiana pressed for full independence. But some residents of the territory feared independence. They believed that a new government might seize their property or that social and economic turmoil might result. Many families moved to Europe to seek work or education.

Through the 1960s, Dutch Guiana continued to demand independence. Young adults who had studied in Europe returned to support this effort. Independence leaders formed the Nationalist Republican Party (PNR). This party pressed for an absolute end to foreign control of Dutch Guiana.

In 1973 a Creole leader named Henck Arron was elected as prime minister (head of government, or chief decision-making authority) of Dutch Guiana. Arron was the leader of the PNR. He made alliances with the other political parties to ensure cooperation among the territory's ethnic groups. And he immediately began discussing terms of independence with the government of the Netherlands. On November 25, 1975, the Republic of Suriname finally won its independence.

A legislature called the National Assembly met to debate and pass laws. Johan Ferrier, a former colonial governor, served as Suriname's first president (head of state, or chief public representative). Arron continued as prime minister. Arron won reelection to the post in 1977.

The Dutch government promised generous financial aid to help Suriname attract investment. The aid depended on Suriname's progress in building democracy (government by freely elected representatives) and a free-market economy.

**Henck Arron** gives a speech as prime minister of Suriname in the late 1970s.

## ◉ Military Rule

In the late 1970s, Suriname had a weak government. Its many political factions were in constant conflict. Foreign companies, unsure of Suriname's future, were reluctant to invest there. Dogged by unemployment and poverty, many Surinamese moved to the Netherlands.

The discontent fueled a revolt in Suriname's military. On February 25, 1980, a group of sixteen military officers overthrew the government. They suspended the constitution and the legislature. They formed a military junta (ruling committee) called the National Military Council.

**Dési Bouterse**

Dési Bouterse headed the junta. A civilian president still served as head of state, but Bouterse controlled the government behind the scenes.

At first people welcomed the change. They thought it would end government corruption and improve the economy. But the junta quickly grew unpopular. It began arresting opponents and censoring the media. Protesters demanded that the junta step down and restore Suriname's constitution.

To calm the protests, the junta set up a group of military and civilian leaders called the Revolutionary People's Front. But few Surinamese supported the Front as a return to democracy. In 1982 Bouterse announced plans to hold an election. Meanwhile, the junta increased pressure on its opponents.

On the night of December 8, 1982, officials brought sixteen captives—fourteen civilians and two soldiers who had spoken out against the junta—to Paramaribo's Fort Zeelandia. All but one of the captives were tortured and executed.

In response to these killings, the United States and the Netherlands halted financial aid to and trade with Suriname. The country's export-driven economy ground nearly to a halt.

Many Surinamese blamed Bouterse personally for the murders. Strikes and protests took place in the streets of the capital. The junta responded by shutting down newspapers, silencing radio stations, and arresting demonstrators.

The Netherlands and the United States pressured the junta to name civilians to lead government departments. Political leaders began discussing a new constitution. In late 1985, the reinstated National Assembly approved a constitution placing power firmly in the hands of civilian leaders. The government scheduled a public vote on the constitution for 1987.

A soldier of Brunswijk's **Suriname National Liberation Army** arrests a man accused of looting during unrerst in 1986.

## Jungle Rebellion

At the same time, a revolt against the military government was brewing in the interior. A Maroon militia (informal army) formed around Ronnie Brunswijk. The junta had stripped Brunswijk of his post as a bodyguard for Bouterse. Brunswijk's loss of rank and power prompted him to take up arms against the regime.

Brunswijk named his militia the Suriname National Liberation Army. Many also knew it as the Jungle Commando. Frequent clashes broke out between the militia and the Surinamese army. The army swept through the countryside, destroying villages and killing people believed to support the rebels. Many people living in eastern Suriname fled to French Guiana.

Growing ever more unpopular, the regime allowed the appointment of a civilian prime minister. In 1987 voters overwhelmingly approved the new constitution. It established the president, not the prime minister, as the nation's chief decision maker. In the fall of that year, the National Assembly elected Ramsewak Shankar as Suriname's new civilian president.

To settle the conflict in the countryside, the new government and the Jungle Commando signed a peace treaty called the Kourou Accord in 1989. But Bouterse, who still led the military, blocked efforts to carry out the treaty's provisions. Bouterse denounced the provision that made Jungle Commando members police officers in areas of the country inhabited mostly by Maroons. So the fighting continued.

Bouterse and the junta were not ready to completely surrender power. In December 1990, Bouterse telephoned President Shankar, demanding that he resign. Fearing for his life, Shankar did. After this "telephone coup," the legislature approved a new president selected by the junta, Johan Kraag.

Under pressure from the United States and the United Nations, the junta held National Assembly elections in spring 1991. The Suriname National Party (NPS), the Progressive Reform Party (VHP), the Indonesian Peasants Party (KTPI), and the Surinamese Labor Party (SPA) joined forces to form the New Front for Democracy and Development. This coalition held a majority of seats in the legislature. In September 1991, the National Assembly elected Ronald Venetiaan of the NPS as Suriname's new president.

The government signed another peace treaty with the Jungle Commando in August 1992. In 1993 Bouterse gave up leadership of Suriname's military. His replacement, Arthy Gorre, brought the army under the government's control. Bouterse helped establish the National Democratic Party (NDP) to peacefully oppose the New Front Coalition.

## ▶ Economic Challenges

After Bouterse stepped down, foreign trade and investment resumed. But the decade-long Dutch and U.S. trade ban had done serious economic damage. Rising government debt lowered the value of Suriname's currency. As the nation's money lost its value, prices for goods and services rose.

In response, Suriname cut public spending. And gradually, as Suriname's export sector revived, the economy improved. The Netherlands held back some of the aid it had promised at independence, though. The Dutch government put several conditions on further aid. Suriname had to keep spending under control and cooperate in deciding how the money would be used.

Despite the improving economy, the New Front Coalition lost popularity. In 1996 elections gave the NDP, still led by Bouterse, the most legislative seats. The NDP joined forces with several smaller parties in the National Assembly. This coalition elected Jules Wijdenbosch president of Suriname.

Suriname's economy remained fragile from years of political turmoil and violence. The Wijdenbosch government could not control public spending or convince the Netherlands to resume full investment in Suriname. Most of the country's natural resources, such as timber and minerals, needed foreign money for development. Limited foreign investment meant that very few big businesses could run profitably or hire new workers.

More than twenty thousand protesters gathered in Paramaribo during a **1999 demonstration against rising prices and unemployment.**

In 1999 thousands of people took to the streets of Paramaribo. They protested the lack of jobs and the rising prices of food and basic goods. In response, the government scheduled early legislative elections.

## Twenty-First Century Suriname

Elections took place in spring 2000. The New Front Coalition regained control of the assembly. This coalition returned Venetiaan to the presidency.

In addition to economic problems, Venetiaan's government faced a border dispute with Guyana. The two nations argued over which tributary of the Corantijn River forms the southern reaches of their shared border. The nations also disagreed on how their border extends into the coastal waters.

The dispute disrupted offshore oil drilling in an area claimed by both countries. In 2004 Suriname sent small gunboats to force out a Canadian oil-exploration company hired by Guyana. Suriname and Guyana later resolved the maritime dispute through the United Nations. But the countries still argue over fishing rights, cross-border traffic, and the location of their southern border.

**President Ronald Venetiaan** arrives at a 2009 pan-American meeting on energy and the environment.

In the 2005 legislative elections, voters still unhappy about the economy defeated the New Front Coalition. But after much wrangling among political parties, the National Assembly returned Venetiaan to the presidency.

In 2007 thousands of teachers, bus drivers, and farmworkers walked off their jobs. A rolling strike had been affecting different sectors of the economy for three years. Striking workers refused to work for a set amount of time, then returned to work. The strike affected different industries at different times. The rolling strike kept constant pressure on employers and the government. The strikers wanted better pay raises. Their wages were not keeping up with the rising cost of living. Surinamese workers also wanted the government to address rising food and energy prices.

Despite ongoing inflation, Suriname's economy has improved since military rule ended. The country has become more self-sufficient in food and basic consumer goods. In search of new export income, Suriname has offered mining and oil exploration leases to foreign firms. It has set aside several large nature preserves. A developing tourist industry is bringing in visitors and helping the economy.

Suriname continues to have mixed relations with the Netherlands. Dutch courts have charged Bouterse for the December 1982 massacre. But by Surinamese law, Suriname cannot extradite him (send him out of the country), because he is a former head of government. These legal issues complicate political and economic relations between the two nations. In 2008 Suriname brought Bouterse to trial for the 1982 killings. This trial continued into 2009.

## Government

Suriname governs itself by the constitution of 1987. This document divides government powers among the legislative, executive, and judicial branches.

The National Assembly is Suriname's unicameral (one-chamber) legislature. Citizens elect fifty-one representatives every five years. All adults eighteen years or older have the right to vote. A Council of State reviews—and has the power to veto—laws passed by the National Assembly.

Every five years, after the legislative elections, the National Assembly members elect a president. If no presidential candidate wins two-thirds of the National Assembly votes, the presidential election goes to a People's Assembly. The People's Assembly includes National Assembly members and local representatives.

The president heads Suriname's executive branch. The president is both head of state and head of government. He or she appoints a cabinet of ministers. The cabinet includes seventeen members who head the various government departments.

The Court of Justice is the highest court in Suriname. The president appoints its members, who serve for life. Suriname also has local courts, where judges called magistrates preside.

Suriname divides its land into ten districts. Districts are regional divisions similar to U.S. states. A commissioner appointed by the president heads each district. The districts are further divided into sixty-two resorts.

Visit www.vgsbooks.com for links to websites with additional information about the history and government of Suriname, including news from the National Assembly.

# THE PEOPLE

Suriname is home to 492,829 people. The population is growing slowly, at the rate of 1.1 percent per year. But researchers expect the population to start shrinking. Suriname's birthrate is slowing. And Suriname loses many young people to the Netherlands and other European nations, where job opportunities are better. The projected population for 2050 is 462,000—a loss of 8 percent.

Suriname's population density is 8 people per square mile (3 people per square km). It's one of the world's least crowded nations overall. The Surinamese inhabit their country unevenly. More than 90 percent of the people live near the northern coast. As a result, the southern population is very sparse.

Since the mid-1900s, the population of Suriname has been changing steadily from rural to urban. In 1950 about 53 percent of Surinamese lived in rural areas, while 47 percent lived in cities. Sixty years later, only 24 percent of Surinamese live in rural areas, while 76 percent live in cities.

## Ethnic Groups

Several different ethnic groups live in Suriname. All but a few descend from colonial-era immigrants.

South Asian Indians form the largest ethnic group. They make up 37 percent of Suriname's population. Surinamese Indians began arriving in 1873. In modern Suriname, Indians are still largely employed as farmers and plantation workers.

About 31 percent of the population is Creole. Creoles descend from West African slaves and European colonists. This ethnic group played an important role in Suriname's drive for independence. The Creoles form a majority in Suriname's cities.

Javanese people make up about 15 percent of the population. This ethnic group is another community descended from late colonial contract workers. In modern Suriname, the Javanese are struggling to preserve their culture. They speak a dialect of Javanese and follow a religion that combines aspects of Christianity, Buddhism, and Islam. The Javanese in

**Young Javanese women** practice a traditional dance form at a school in Paramaribo. Such schools help preserve Javanese customs in Suriname.

Suriname have also preserved art forms such as gamelan music (performed by an orchestra of gongs, xylophones, drums, and more) and *wayang kulit* (shadow puppetry).

Many people in small rural communities descend from slaves who escaped the colonial plantations. These Maroon communities make up 10 percent of the population. Maroons belong to several distinct groups, such as Aukaner, Boni, Saramaccan, Paramaccan, Matawari, and Kwinti. Most live by small-scale farming, hunting, and trading.

The Maroons of Suriname are matrilineal. They trace their ancestry through their mothers. But men have always served as *gammans* (chiefs) in Maroon societies. Times are slowly changing. In 1995 members of the Ndjuka community elected the first female Maroon *kabiten* (village leader).

Indigenous peoples form 2 percent of Suriname's population. A few thousand Caribs and Arawaks live in northern Suriname. The Trió and the Wayana, who number several hundred each, live in the rain forests of the south and southeast. Other smaller groups make up the rest of Suriname's indigenous population.

Suriname's Chinese population has reached 2 percent of the population. The first Chinese workers came before the end of slavery. After their contracts expired, most of the Chinese returned home. The rest moved to Paramaribo, where many intermarried with the city's Creoles. The Chinese worked as traders and merchants. They still make up a sizable community in the capital.

About 1 percent of Surinamese are white people of European

descent. These people, called Boeroes, descend from Suriname's Dutch colonists. The Dutch keep strong ties with the Netherlands. Many Boeroes have family on both sides of the Atlantic Ocean.

The name Boeroes comes from the Dutch word *boer*, which means "farmer." A similar name survives in South Africa, where the Dutch also settled. South Africans of Dutch descent are called Boers.

Other ethnic groups form the remaining 2 percent of Suriname's population. In recent years, Suriname has seen an influx of Brazilians. Many of these people come to mine for gold in the hills and streams of Suriname's rain forests. These *garimpeiros* (self-employed gold miners) live apart from Surinamese culture and governance. They trade in gold and speak Portuguese, the language of Brazil.

## ▶ Health

Many health problems in Suriname arise from poor sanitation. Poor sanitation often leads to polluted water and the spread of diseases, such as cholera (a deadly diarrheal infection) and typhus (a dangerous illness carried by body lice).

Dengue and malaria are common in Suriname. Mosquitoes spread both diseases. Dengue is a painful and disabling—but rarely fatal—disease. Malaria causes extreme weakness and pain, and sometimes

A Trió family from southern Suriname poses with a pet monkey.

Volunteers hand out information and collect donations at a popular beach near Paramaribo during an **AIDS prevention campaign.**

brain damage and death. These illnesses affect many Surinamese children. No medicines exist to treat dengue. Medicines that used to work against malaria are losing their effectiveness. Bed nets, which protect people from mosquitoes at night, are the most effective means to prevent both diseases.

The average Surinamese man can expect to live 66 years. The average woman can expect to live 73 years. The leading causes of death for adults are cancer, heart disease, and stroke. Suriname faces a rising rate of acquired immunodeficiency syndrome (AIDS), a disease caused by the human immunodeficiency virus (HIV). HIV spreads by sexual contact and the use of contaminated drug needles. About 1.9 percent of Surinamese between the ages of 15 and 49 years carry HIV. It has become a major cause of death for people in this age group.

In Suriname about 16 of every 1,000 babies die before the age of one year. This infant mortality rate is lower than Guyana's but higher than French Guiana's. Suriname's rate is about four times higher than that of the Netherlands.

Suriname has 1 doctor for every 2,000 people. The country spends 8 percent of its gross domestic product (GDP) on health care. (The GDP is the total value of goods and services produced inside the country.)

In a drive to improve public health, the government has allowed nongovernmental organizations (NGOs) to set up health clinics where they're most needed. Childhood vaccination programs help prevent measles and typhus. The government extends some financial help to people who are disabled and to senior citizens living in poverty. Free medical services are available to the poor.

## Education

Suriname requires children to attend six years of primary school (elementary school) starting at age seven. After finishing sixth grade, students take an examination. This test places students in their next course of study at junior high school. Junior high school lasts four years. It offers courses in Dutch, English, Spanish, accounting, mathematics, physics, biology, geography, history, drawing, and physical education. A senior high school of three years follows.

About 97 percent of children eligible for primary school attend classes. About 75 percent of eligible children attend secondary school. Teachers instruct in Dutch—a second language for most students. Suriname's overall rate of adult literacy (the ability to read and write) is 90 percent.

Some private schools teach in English. Many are Christian schools that attract large numbers of Creole students. The government supports these schools. Both public schools and private schools in Suriname offer their courses free of charge.

Vocational and technical schools offer adults training in education, health care, and other occupations. Anton de Kom University of Suriname in Paramaribo was founded in 1968. It is the country's only university. It offers degrees in medicine, law, engineering, environmental studies, business, and public administration.

Children of the Galibi group attend primary school in their village near the Galibi Nature Reserve.

## Women in Suriname

Surinamese women of all ethnic groups tend to hold a traditional role in the home, caring for their families. Especially before independence, few women were involved in government or business. A small number worked in factories, service industries, or mining. Some were teachers or nurses.

Since 1948 adult women in Suriname have had the right to vote and to run for public office. But Suriname's drive for independence in the 1960s and 1970s included no female politicians or labor leaders. In the 1980s, the climate began to change for women. They united to protest the harsh rule of the military junta. The economic problems of the 1980s and 1990s placed many women at the political forefront.

By the early twenty-first century, about 20 percent of Surinamese legislators were women. The first female judge was appointed to the Court of Justice, the country's highest court, in 2001. The country's new constitution extends legal protection against gender discrimination. The law guarantees equal access to education and jobs. It also allows women to inherit property.

Despite this progress, women still have a lower literacy rate than men do in Suriname. Many young girls do not attend school past the primary years. In addition, health care for expectant mothers remains inadequate in many places. This situation places both mothers and their infants at risk.

Visit www.vgsbooks.com for links to websites with additional information about the people of Suriname, including the latest information on efforts to improve health care in rural areas.

## Family Life

In many Surinamese families, parents select spouses for their children. This practice is particularly common among Indian families. Most Surinamese marry within their own ethnic group. Weddings are occasions for elaborate feasts and parties.

Most Surinamese live in nuclear families. Nuclear families are households made up of just parents and their children. The divorce rate in Suriname is high. Single women head about 30 percent of households. Babies sleep with mothers until they can walk. Once a baby is mobile, he or she moves to a separate room—if one is available. In some rural homes, a single room serves as living and sleeping quarters for the entire family.

In this **extended Maroon family**, grandparents live together with their children and grandchildren.

Among the Maroon people, some men practice polygamy. They have two or more wives who live in different households, often in different villages. The husband provides a home and land for his wives to farm. A group of Maroon families who descend from a single female ancestor is called an *io,* or clan. Members of the same clan may not intermarry. In some Maroon villages, residents belong to the same clan.

Both Maroon and indigenous families hold initiation rites as their children enter adolescence. Among the Wayana, for example, boys must endure the stinging of wasps. Caribs hold a similar rite using fierce red ants for girls.

## CHANGING TIMES

In Suriname's interior, people tend to live in isolated villages. They have little contact with the outside world—mainly by radio and mobile telephone. They have few visitors. As a result of their isolation, many interior communities have unique cultures and language dialects. They are typically completely self-sufficient.

But Suriname is beginning to open its savanna and rain forest regions to tourists. The nation is creating large nature parks and animal reserves to attract visitors. As more people venture inland, they disrupt long-standing indigenous and Maroon lands, cultures, and economies.

# CULTURAL LIFE

Suriname's cultural life reflects influences from all over the world. People from South America, the Caribbean, North America, Europe, Africa, and South Asia have all contributed to Surinamese customs.

## ▶ Religion

Suriname has no official religion. The nation is home to many different religious beliefs and practices. About 41 percent of Surinamese are Christian. About 20 percent are Hindu, 14 percent are Muslim, and 3 percent practice traditional religions (animism). About 18 percent follow other religions, and 4 percent are atheists, meaning they do not believe in any god.

Dutch colonists first brought Christianity to Suriname. Many modern Surinamese have accepted the Christian faith through missionaries (religious teachers). About half of Surinamese Christians are Protestants. The other half are mostly Roman Catholics. A few are Mormons, who belong to the Church of Jesus Christ of Latter-day

Saints. They follow the teachings of the American prophet (spiritual spokesperson) Joseph Smith.

Indian workers brought Hinduism to Suriname. Hinduism is a religion based on four ancient texts called Vedas, compiled in about 1200 B.C. Each Veda is a collection of hymns, prayers, and rituals. Unlike other major world religions, Hinduism has no single founder. In Hinduism divine power takes the shape of three main gods: Brahma, the creator; Vishnu, the preserver; and Shiva, the destroyer. Individual Hindus choose their own forms of worship.

Most Muslims in Suriname are descendants of immigrants from Java or India. Suriname has the highest percentage of Muslims among all nations in the Americas. Islam is a religion founded by the Arab prophet Muhammad in the A.D. 600s. Muslims believe that Allah (God) gave messages to Muhammad through the angel Gabriel. The holy scriptures of the Koran contain these messages. Muslims strive to fulfill the five pillars (central duties) of Islam: faith in Allah; giving charity; praying

**An indigenous spiritual leader** performs a ritual in Paramaribo.

five times daily; fasting during the holy month of Ramadan; and visiting the holy city of Mecca, Saudi Arabia, once in a lifetime, if possible.

Surinamese indigenous peoples and Maroons typically practice animism. Animism's central belief is that spirits live in all things—people, animals, plants, and the natural world. It also teaches that dead ancestors are spiritually alive. Spirits may be good or evil, and they can affect human lives and events. For animists, keeping the spirits in balance is very important. Shamans (spiritual healers) perform rituals or prescribe remedies to restore health, protect against evil spirits, and bring good fortune. Maroons use the *kwinti* rite to honor their ancestors. Many Surinamese blend animism with Christianity.

## ◉ Languages

Since colonial times, Suriname's official language has been Dutch. It is the main language in schools, in government affairs, and in broadcast and print media. But despite its long usage, most Surinamese speak Dutch as a second—not first—language. Dutch is less common inland and in rural areas. Many indigenous Surinamese don't speak Dutch at all.

Most Surinamese speak Sranan Tongo (Suriname Tongue) as a first or second language. Sranan blends African languages, English, Portuguese, and Dutch. This blending makes Sranan useful

Surinamese Creoles greet each other with the phrase *no span!* (Everything's cool!) They take a relaxed attitude toward life's challenges. Good friends hug. Everyone shakes hands. A dinner invitation is a common way to end a conversation. That evening the guests arrive— usually walking right in without knocking.

for communication among different ethnic groups. During the drive for independence, many Surinamese spoke Sranan as a way of separating themselves from the Dutch. Dési Bouterse was the first political leader to use Sranan in public speeches.

Each Maroon community has a language of its own. The Maroon tongues include Saramaccan, Kwinti, and Aukan. These cultures began in isolation, and over the years their members developed their own vocabulary.

Suriname's indigenous communities also have their own languages, such as Akurio, Arawak, Carib, Sikiana, Trió, Warao, and Wayana. Few people outside the Guiana region know these languages.

The Indian people of Suriname speak a language called Sarnami Hindi. It is distantly related to the language their ancestors spoke in northern India.

The Javanese people of Suriname speak Suriname Javanese. This language is related to—but quite different from—the Javanese dialect spoken in Indonesia.

Surinamese people of Chinese heritage use the Hakka dialect. Linguists trace Hakka to the southeastern provinces of China. This region was the homeland of most Chinese immigrants to Suriname.

Some Surinamese argue that English should become the nation's official language. In their opinion, even though English is not in common use, it would help citizens overcome ethnic divisions. It would also tie Suriname more closely to the Caribbean and North America.

Signs in Suriname often use both **Dutch and English text.** Most people understand at least one of the languages.

**A storyteller of the Trió people** holds a parrot while telling a folktale.

## ▶ Literature

Long before colonial settlement, Suriname's indigenous people created a storytelling tradition. They recited tales and myths from memory and passed them along from one generation to the next. Frederik and Arthur Penard were the first to collect these tales in a book: *The Man-Eating Worshippers of the Sunsnake*, published in 1907.

The colonists began a Surinamese literary tradition in Dutch. *Cudjo the Firebrand*, a historical novel by H. F. Rikken, found a wide audience in the first decade of the 1900s. Jacques Samuels wrote the popular *Sketches and Characters of Suriname*, a nonfiction book about the colony's people and history, in the 1940s.

In modern Suriname, the publishing industry is very small. Many writers simply print their own works and give them to friends, or sell the works through bookshops in Paramaribo.

Modern Surinamese literature includes poetry, novels, short stories, and children's books. Suriname celebrates its poets, especially Robin Ravales. Ravales wrote under the pen name Dobru. He often performed his work in public. His poetry became famous throughout the Guiana region, the Caribbean, and the Netherlands during the 1970s. He wrote his best-known poem, "Wan Bon" ("One Tree"), in 1965. It describes Suriname's multiethnic society.

Gerrit Barron and Ismene Krishnadath are noted Surinamese children's authors. Cynthia McLeod writes adult fiction based on Surinamese history. Her book *Twice Marienburg* tells the story of an important sugar plantation and its employees in the early 1900s.

# Music

The music of Suriname shows many different influences. For indigenous villages of the interior, music is a key part of public celebrations. The Wayana, for example, gather to hear the *kalau*, a chant that relays the story of their origins. To provide rhythm and melody for public dances, Wayana musicians use bamboo flutes, turtle shells, rattles, and heavy stamping sticks.

Among the Arawaks, who live closer to urban Suriname, traditional songs and dances are slowly dying out. The Arawaks have adopted the guitar and often use this instrument with flutes and drums to perform *kawina* music. Kawina is a style borrowed from Suriname's Creoles.

In traditional kawina music, large drum ensembles accompany singers and dancers. The music developed in the late 1800s, after Suriname's slaves won their freedom. It took many features directly from West African music. *Kaseko* is another musical style popular among Creoles. This dance music combines the complex rhythms of Africa with popular music from the United States and Europe. Kaseko bands include saxophones, trumpets, guitars, and several percussion instruments.

Caribbean styles such as reggae and calypso have a wide audience along the seacoast. Music clubs regularly feature calypso stars, as well as salsa bands from elsewhere in South America. Soul, funk, and rock and roll from the United States have been popular in Suriname since the 1960s.

Members of the **Aukaner Maroons dance to traditional music** based on African rhythms.

Surinamese emigrants have influenced the music of the Netherlands. The Suriname Troubadours and other groups have entered the Dutch musical mainstream. Europe, in turn, has shared its love for jazz with Suriname. Paramaribo holds a big jazz festival every October.

Asian immigrants have also influenced Suriname's music scene. People of Indian heritage throughout the Caribbean celebrate the songs of Ramdew Chaitoe. Chaitoe adapted Afro-Caribbean rhythms to Hindu devotional songs, creating a lively and unique sound called chutney.

The Javanese of Suriname brought their musical traditions as well. Traditional gamelan music accompanies wayang kulit performances. The gamelan's many pitches and tones weave long threads of complex, hypnotic rhythm.

# Art and Architecture

Suriname lacks formal art schools. Many Surinamese artists study in the Netherlands. Sculptor Erwin de Vries did so in the 1950s. In 2002 he created a monument for Amsterdam, a large city in the Netherlands. The monument recalled the history of slavery in the Dutch colonies.

Painters Rinaldo Klas, Kurt Nahar, and Marcel Pinas all studied in Jamaica. Klas creates art inspired by Suriname's natural environment. Nahar's subject matter is the often-violent history of Suriname. Pinas's work draws on Maroon culture.

Many Maroons are skillful wood-carvers. They make a variety of household and personal items by shaping natural wood with knives, adzes, and planes. Maroon carvers also decorate gourd utensils with natural forms or geometric designs. Maroon women use a dye-and-wax method called batik. This craft, which originated in Indonesia, creates colorful skirts, blouses, and turbans.

Arawaks and Caribs use clay to fashion small pottery items.

A Saramaccan Maroon man displays a carved **wooden tabletop.**

They make necklaces and other ornaments out of shells and beads. The Javanese also specialize in batik, as well as basketry and making shadow puppets. These delicate puppets are made of thin wood and paper.

Suriname's architecture has a distinctive Dutch flavor. Colonial settlers built wood and brick homes with pitched roofs—much like houses in the Netherlands. Surinamese homes are usually painted white, with green door and window frames and red-brick foundations. Balconies and long porches offer a place to enjoy cool evenings.

## Sports

Suriname's most popular sport is *voetbal* (soccer). The country has a twelve-team national league, the Surinaamse Voetbal Bond. The league formed in 1924. Its teams compete every year for the President's Cup. The Robinhood squad, Suriname's best, has claimed twenty-three titles in its history.

Suriname has contributed many soccer players to the Netherlands and other European nations. These include Frank Rijkaard, Patrick Kluivert, Aron Winter, Edgar Davids, and Ryan Babel.

Suriname can boast of stars in other sports too. For example, Primraj Binda, Tommy Asinga, and Letitia Vriesde were all top-rated track athletes. Swimmer Anthony Nesty is Suriname's only Olympic medalist. For the 100-meter butterfly, he won a gold medal at the 1988 games in Seoul, South Korea, and a bronze medal at the 1992 games in Barcelona, Spain. Nesty coached Suriname's swim team at the 2008 Olympic games in Beijing, China.

Surinamese player **Frank Rijkaard** scores for the Holland International team in a 1988 game.

The English game of cricket is gaining popularity in Suriname. This baseball-like game has long been popular in Caribbean nations that were once British colonies. Suriname's national cricket team began competing in regional matches in 2004.

Suriname hosts an international auto rally every November. This long-distance race is called the Suriname Savannah Rally. It lasts four days. It challenges four-wheel-drive vehicles to race on rough terrain from the coast into the savanna. Teams from Europe, the Caribbean, and the United States compete.

## Holidays and Festivals

Suriname's many ethnic groups have crowded the national calendar with holidays. These include both religious and secular celebrations.

Indian Arrival Day occurs on June 5. This holiday celebrates the immigration of Indian workers to Suriname. The Indian community celebrates Divali in October or November (dates vary). This five-day Hindu festival marks the start of the Hindu new year and symbolizes the victory of good over evil. During Divali people light tiny clay oil lamps and place them on houses and temples or set them adrift on rivers.

Christmas and Easter are public holidays in Suriname. The day after Christmas is Boxing Day, a day for gift giving. Suriname's key Muslim holidays are Eid al-Fitr and Eid al-Adha. Muslim holidays follow a lunar calendar, so their dates change each year. Eid al-Fitr happens at the end

**Christians celebrate Palm Sunday,** the Sunday before Easter, at Saint Alphons Church in Paramaribo.

People set off long strings of firecrackers during a **New Year's celebration** in the streets of Paramaribo.

of the holy month of Ramadan. During the daylight hours of Ramadan, Muslims fast (avoid eating and drinking) to honor Allah's revelation of the Koran to Muhammad. On Eid al-Fitr, Muslims celebrate with feasting, praying, and family gatherings. Eid al-Adha honors the biblical Abraham's willingness to sacrifice his son to God.

The Javanese honor births, deaths, marriages, and other important events with ritual meals called *slametans*. Guests are all men. A member of the host household invites guests personally, just a few minutes before the gathering begins. They stop working immediately and gather in the host's home. The host delivers a welcome speech. Everyone joins in a prayer from the Koran. Then the women of the household serve food and tea. In a very short time, the guests politely take their leave.

The Javanese celebrate their Arrival Day on August 9. The Day of Indigenous People takes place one day earlier (August 8).

Oud Jaar (Old Year) is Suriname's national New Year's celebration. It begins on December 31, the last day of the passing year. City streets teem with crowds eating, drinking, and lighting firecrackers. Surifesta, a national festival that runs through December and January, offers concerts, parades, and public gatherings in several cities. Many Surinamese who live abroad return home each year for this event.

Surifesta began in 1981 at a little café called T'Vat in downtown Paramaribo. The party grew each year, moving into the nearby streets and drawing bigger and bigger crowds. Eventually, the little New Year's party became a month-long national celebration of music, dance, and food.

May 1 is Suriname's Labor Day. Kawina, or Emancipation Day, occurs on July 1. This day celebrates the end of slavery in Suriname. A big parade winds through Paramaribo, and swimmers compete in an 11-mile (18 km) race in the Suriname River. To mark the day, Creole women wear the *kata*, a traditional dress that symbolizes escape from slavery.

Srefidensi, or Independence Day, occurs on November 25. This holiday marks the day in 1975 when Suriname won independence from the Netherlands.

Visit www.vgsbooks.com for links to websites with additional information about the culture of Suriname, including recipes for Surinamese food.

## Food

The food of Suriname, like other aspects of Surinamese culture, is ethnically diverse. The national cuisine has roots in Indian, Dutch, West African, Chinese, and Indonesian cooking.

The Javanese community has contributed many Indonesian flavors and cooking methods to Suriname. Spicy meat accompanies fried rice and noodle dishes. Fried, grilled, and stewed fish also appear on the table. On the street *warungs* (food stalls) offer passersby *bami goreng* (fried noodles). Popular refreshments are ginger beer and tart, red sorrel tea. In Suriname sorrel is the name for hibiscus leaves.

Peanut soup and *pasteri*, a chicken-and-vegetable pie, are common Creole dishes. Creole cooks favor plantains (a kind of banana), cassava, and sweet potatoes as side dishes for main courses of chicken and seafood. *Pom* is a popular side dish made from mashed, spiced taro (a starchy edible root).

Bean sprouts top a spicy **Javanese noodle dish** from Suriname.

Suriname's Indian community enjoys traditional curry dishes and roti (small, round flatbread). Indian cooks are also famous for their tandoori dishes, cooked in wood-fired clay ovens.

Rice and beans are Suriname's staple foods. They serve as a base for *moksie alesie*, a stew of chicken, peppers, and tomatoes. Pepper pot is another common stew, made with cassava, marinated meat, and hot peppers. Coconut milk often flavors main meals and desserts.

**Residents of the Javanese Blauwgroud neighborhood of Paramaribo are known for their spicy, delicious cooking. Ordinary families often whip up meals and serve them for a small fee to passersby on their front porches or patios. No tipping necessary!**

# SURINAMESE SPICY FRIED RICE

The Surinamese often serve fried rice alongside chicken and *petjel* (cooked vegetables with peanut sauce). There are many variations of fried rice, so feel free to make changes if you like. For instance, you can add more or less red pepper, depending on how hot you like it.

3 tablespoons vegetable oil

1 small onion, chopped fine

3 cloves garlic, minced

1 teaspoon ground galangal root (optional, available in Asian groceries)

1 tablespoon soy sauce

1½ cups cooked, cooled rice

1 cup celery, chopped fine

1 teaspoon ground hot red pepper, such as cayenne

2 cups vegetable broth

1. Heat oil in a wok or frying pan. Fry onion and garlic on high heat for 1 minute, stirring constantly.
2. Add galangal root and soy sauce. Fry another minute, while stirring.
3. Add rice. Stir-fry the rice until hot and coated with sauce.
4. Add chopped celery and red pepper.
5. Add vegetable broth. Bring to boil. Turn heat down, and simmer for about 15 minutes, or until the rice has absorbed the liquid.

Serves 4.

# THE ECONOMY

At the beginning of the twenty-first century, Suriname's economy was in trouble. The country suffered high unemployment and inflation. Prices were rising 100 percent per year. In addition, the government was spending much more than it took in from taxes and state-owned companies. This budget deficit forced Suriname to borrow money from abroad.

The government tackled its deficit by selling off state-owned companies and raising taxes. The currency stabilized, and prices for goods steadied. By 2007 inflation had slowed to 6.4 percent. Production of goods was growing at a rate of 5 percent per year. The GDP was $4.24 billion, or about $8,900 per person.

Although manufacturing and services are growing, Suriname still depends heavily on mining. Bauxite and gold account for most of Suriname's exports and a large portion of government income. But this reliance on mining puts Suriname at the mercy of rising and falling mineral prices.

To improve its economic outlook, Suriname is letting foreign

companies invest in coastal oil exploration. With oil prices likely to stay high, the energy sector offers Suriname a promise of more stable export earnings in the future.

## ◉ Services

Suriname's service sector encompasses all business activity that provides useful labor instead of material goods. This sector includes banking, insurance, business services, construction, real estate, wholesale and retail trade, transportation, telecommunications, tourism, hotels, bars, restaurants, and government services. This sector accounts for about 65 percent of Suriname's GDP. It employs 78 percent of Surinamese workers.

Services are gradually replacing industry and agriculture. Service businesses generally provide a higher standard of living for workers. But because many youths leave Suriname after finishing school, the country lacks enough workers to help the sector grow quickly.

# ▷ Tourism

Suriname is starting to attract tourists with its wealth of natural beauty and lively culture. In the early twenty-first century, many new hotels have opened in Paramaribo. Many residents of the capital rent their homes to visitors too. From 2005 to 2006, Suriname doubled its number of tourists. This sector continues to grow.

Tourism has developed slowly in Suriname, compared to other Caribbean nations. Unlike its neighbors, Suriname has few natural sand beaches to draw snowbirds from colder climes. It must rely on other attractions, such as the Amazon rain forest of the south. This dense forest remains largely untouched by outsiders.

More than a dozen nature reserves offer hiking, camping, birdwatching, kayaking, fishing, and other activities. Raleigh Vallen (Raleigh Falls) on the Coppename River is one of the most popular destinations. This landmark lies within the Central Suriname Nature Reserve. The same reserve contains Tafel Berg, a famous *tepui* (flattopped mountain). This mountain lies near the remote headwaters of the Saramacca River.

Ecotourism is gaining in popularity. Ecotourism draws visitors who want to enjoy and help protect Suriname's flora, fauna, and cultural heritage. This type of tourism helps Suriname earn income without destroying its resources. Ecotourists can learn about Suriname's rain forest and the impact of mining and development. They can also visit Maroon and indigenous villages. To witness life in these villages, visitors must travel hundreds of miles by bush plane (small, rugged airplane) or by rough forest trails. The history of Suriname is on display at Laarwijk, a colonial plantation in the Commewijne district of northeastern Suriname.

**Tourists snap photos** from a canoe on a tour of the Suriname River.

# Industry

Suriname's industrial sector includes mining, manufacturing, and energy. This sector contributes about 24 percent of the nation's GDP. It employs 14 percent of the labor force.

Suriname is one of the world's largest sources of bauxite. The nation has been mining bauxite since 1918. Its largest mines, which include the mine at Lelydorp, are becoming less productive. To replace them, new bauxite mines at Klaverblad and Kaaimangrasie opened in 2006. Mining engineers have found bauxite deposits at remote sites in eastern and western Suriname too.

Suriname also has large deposits of gold. The nation is beginning to develop large-scale gold mining. But much of the nation's current gold mining is informal. Garimpeiros work alone or in small groups, without government licensing or taxation. They dig along streambeds in the forest of southern Suriname. Their work causes serious chemical pollution in Suriname's rivers.

Refining bauxite into aluminum is Suriname's largest manufacturing industry. The Suriname Aluminum Company (SURALCO), a company owned by ALCOA, is Suriname's major aluminum firm. It operates refining plants in the town of Paranam and other locations.

Small factories operate in Paramaribo and other cities. These plants package farm products such as rice, tobacco, and sugarcane. Busy processing plants make palm oil from coconut and other edible nuts.

## THE TROUBLE WITH MINING

Thousands of Brazilian garimpeiros are mining gold in southeastern Suriname. Logging roads make it easy for them to roam the forest. Armed mining guards prevent local residents from moving about.

The mining process also dumps toxins into the rivers. Many rivers are too acidic to support life. Some carry dangerous amounts of the metallic chemical mercury. Mercury is poisonous. Tiny amounts can cause nerve damage, blindness, deafness, and even death.

Gold miners use liquid mercury to extract gold from soil. They add mercury to the soil. When mercury touches gold, the two substances stick together, making it easier to separate the gold from the dirt.

Commercial gold miners don't usually use mercury. But informal gold miners—like those in Suriname—often do. They release large amounts of mercury into streams and soil. This mercury winds up in the water used by rural people for washing, cooking, and drinking. The mercury also ends up in fish eaten by other animals, including humans.

**The Suriname Aluminum Company** refines bauxite into aluminum at factories like this one.

SURALCO is not only a key manufacturer, but also an important energy firm in Suriname. It owns and operates the hydroelectric plant at Afobaka Dam. Staatsolie, the state-owned oil company, owns the rights to explore and extract Suriname's crude oil reserves. This company has signed partnerships with oil companies in Spain, Denmark, the United States, and Australia. These companies are exploring for offshore oil deposits and building oil refineries onshore.

## ◎ Agriculture

Suriname's agricultural sector includes farming, fishing, and forestry. This sector is responsible for about 11 percent of the nation's GDP. It employs about 8 percent of Surinamese workers.

Suriname has been a productive farming country for more than three centuries. The plantation system once dominated the economy. Surinamese plantations harvested rice, sugarcane, coffee, cotton, and other crops for export to other countries.

Many of the colonial plantations are still running. But their production has dropped from neglect, outdated machinery, poor irrigation, labor shortages, and falling prices on the world market.

Rice is still a key cash crop. It contributes a sizable portion of the country's exports. It can grow throughout the year in Suriname's warm, wet climate, so it is a reliable staple food in city markets. Many families depend on rice both to eat and to sell. But growing rice without machinery requires heavy labor. Rice farmers must also build and maintain paddies (flooded fields) and irrigation canals.

**Two boys show off the rice harvest** from their farm near Nieuw Nickerie.

A state-owned company controls Suriname's sugarcane industry. The company runs a large plantation at Mariënburg. Suriname also has coffee and banana plantations, groves of coconut and citrus trees, and small farms producing corn, tomatoes, plantains, soybeans, peanuts, cabbage, sweet potatoes, and cassava.

The use of Suriname's coastal land for rice and other crops limits the grazing land available for livestock. Cattle breeding is difficult in Suriname. Tropical diseases are common, and dense forest still covers much of the land. Small herds of sheep and goats, as well as chickens and pigs, provide Suriname's meat supply. Because livestock farming is limited, the national diet depends on fruits, vegetables, rice, fish, and seafood instead of meat.

For many coastal towns and villages, fishing is the most important source of income and employment. Fish and shrimp are important agricultural exports. Foreign countries, such as Japan, have invested in commercial fish farms in Suriname.

## FISHING CONTEST

In the boundary waters between Suriname and Guyana, fishing can be a very serious business. Guyanese fishers have been trawling Surinamese waters without licenses and using special fish traps banned in Suriname. This illegal fishing is causing the fish stock to dwindle. It is also harming endangered sea turtles. The Surinamese police and military patrol the coast demanding licenses, inspecting boats, and making arrests. The fishing conflict is one ingredient in the ongoing political tension between Suriname and Guyana.

Virgin (uncut) rain forest still covers more than half of Suriname. In the 1900s, roads began reaching into the interior. These roads gave lumber companies better access to the country's forests. The timber industry grew throughout the twentieth century. But this growth has brought conflict to rural areas. The government rents logging rights to private companies without consulting local residents about their farming and hunting needs. When local villagers and farmers resist logging companies, the government sends in soldiers to support the companies.

## ◉ Foreign Trade

Like many former colonies, Suriname's economy still relies heavily on exports. Aluminum, gold, and oil account for about 85 percent of Suriname's exports. The other 15 percent of exports are mainly rice, bananas, fish, shrimp, and lumber. The country's most important export partners are Norway, the United States, Canada, and France.

Suriname imports heavy machinery, steel, consumer goods, and fuel. The Netherlands, Brazil, and the United States are leading import partners. As part of the Caribbean Community (CARICOM), a trade partnership among Caribbean countries, Suriname enjoys good terms, such as low taxes, for regional imports and exports.

## ◉ Transportation

Suriname's transportation system is underdeveloped. Poor infrastructure (public works such as roads and bridges) hinders the nation's economy.

Suriname's network of roads is sparse. It has about 2,674 miles (4,304 km) of roads in total. About one-quarter of these roads are paved. Most of the roads lie along the northern coast. These roads link Paramaribo and other towns.

In the interior, dense forest makes road building difficult and

### PALM OIL PROBLEMS

Suriname has much undeveloped land—even along the coast. This land has drawn interest from foreign companies seeking to set up new plantations.

For example, the palm oil industry is attracting new investment from India and China. Asian companies are buying up huge tracts of land and planting them with palm trees. The fruits and seeds of these trees produce an oil widely used in foods, soaps, and cosmetics.

Local people in the Marowijne district of northeastern Suriname are resisting the palm plantations. The Surinamese fear foreign companies plan to hire only contract laborers from their own countries.

**Tiny jungle airstrips** serve some of Suriname's most isolated areas.

expensive. Most roads are narrow dirt lanes following the rivers. These routes generally run north and south. Some small car ferries are available. Ferries also bring travelers across the rivers separating Suriname from Guyana and French Guiana.

There are no public railroads in Suriname. The nation's two little-used rail lines once carried mining supplies and ore. New roads made these routes unnecessary, and they fell into disuse.

Johan Adolf Pengel International Airport links Suriname to the Netherlands and destinations in the Caribbean, Brazil, and the United States. Small planes can hop among several airstrips in the south. These small airports provide many communities' only links to the outside world.

## Communications

With Dutch as its official language, Suriname lies outside the Caribbean media mainstream. In this region, the main languages are Spanish, English, and French. Broadcast and print media find it challenging to run in a small market and a country with ongoing economic troubles. Nevertheless, Paramaribo is home to two daily newspapers, *De Ware Tijd* and *De West*.

Suriname's main Dutch-language television station is ATV. It presents news and covers important events. STVS provides music programs, sports coverage, dramas, and other entertainment.

Two women make phone calls outside a **Telesur office** offering Internet access in Nieuw Nickerie.

Radio is the primary source of news and entertainment for most Surinamese. Radio Garuda broadcasts in Javanese and Dutch for the Javanese community. Radio Apintie, whose motto is "The Happy Station," broadcasts pop music over the air and on the Internet.

Eight percent of people regularly access the Internet in Suriname. Many use Internet cafés, where people can rent computer time. About one thousand households and businesses have high-speed Internet access.

Telesur is Suriname's state-owned telecommunications company. About 20 percent of households have landline service. Because the service is costly and unreliable, many Surinamese use mobile telephones instead. Telesur launched a nationwide mobile network in 2002.

## The Future

Since independence in 1975, Suriname has suffered a great deal of economic and political turmoil. Unemployment and inflation have been constant problems. Suriname's many political groups have trouble cooperating with one other. As a result, uncertainty clouds future government policies. Economic aid from the Netherlands and other countries in Europe and the Americas depends on long-term political peace and stability in Suriname.

To bolster its economy, Suriname is turning to other sources of help. It is beginning to attract investment from China and India. These rapidly growing nations are looking for opportunities to set up profitable businesses in countries like Suriname, which have low labor and operating costs. The country still depends heavily on good prices for its mineral exports and crude oil. It needs to diversify its economy. Closer economic cooperation with Asia may provide the variety Suriname needs and balance the nation's cultural and historical ties to Europe.

Visit www.vgsbooks.com for links to websites with additional information about Suriname's economy, including the latest updates on foreign trade and energy resources.

CA. 7000 B.C.  Nomadic hunter-gatherers live in southern Suriname.

CA. 1000 B.C.  Arawaks, Caribs, and other indigenous peoples hunt, fish, and farm along the coast of northern South America.

CA. 0  Ancient farming societies make petroglyphs and burial mounds along the seacoast and in the Corantijn and Marowijne river valleys.

A.D. 1200s  The Arawak people retreat from coastal areas to the interior.

1498  Christopher Columbus sails along the Guiana coast.

1593  Spain claims the territory of Guiana.

1616  Dutch settlers arrive in Guiana.

1630  The first British settlers arrive at Marshall's Creek.

1667  The British trade central Guiana for New Amsterdam (modern Manhattan Island).

1674  The Treaty of Westminster officially makes Dutch Guiana a colony of the Netherlands.

1683  The Dutch government names Cornelis van Aerssen van Sommelsdijk Dutch Guiana's first governor.

1712  French pirate Jacques Cassard and his men rampage through Dutch Guiana.

1780-1815  The British raid and occupy Dutch Guiana almost constantly.

1815  The Treaty of Vienna returns Dutch Guiana permanently to the Netherlands.

1863  Dutch Guiana abolishes slavery. Former slaves must continue paid plantation work for ten years.

1866  The Netherlands grants limited voting rights to tax-paying property owners in Dutch Guiana.

1873  Freed slaves' ten years of required plantation work ends.

LATE 1800s–  Indian, Javanese, and Chinese contract workers arrive in Dutch
EARLY 1900s  Guiana to do plantation work.

1900  A rush of miners to the interior results in rising gold exports from the colony.

1914-1918  World War I raises demand for bauxite. Suriname's first bauxite mines begin operating.

1920s  The Aluminum Company of America buys mining rights and begins refining bauxite into aluminum in Suriname.

1939-1945  World War II sharply raises demand for Dutch Guiana's aluminium.

1945    The Dutch grants Dutch Guiana some self-rule.

1948    Women gain the right to vote and run for public office in Dutch
        Guiana.

1954    Dutch Guiana becomes an autonomous territory. The Netherlands
        keeps control of Dutch Guiana's defense and foreign affairs.

1960s   The Nationalist Republican Party presses for full independence.

1975    The Republic of Suriname wins independence from the Netherlands. Johan
        Ferrier becomes the first president.

1980    Military officers overthrow the government of Suriname. Dési Bouterse leads the
        ruling junta.

1982    The junta arrests, tortures, and executes fifteen political opponents.

1986    Maroon Ronnie Brunswijk forms the Jungle Commando and attacks state-owned tar-
        gets. The government cracks down on rural Maroon communities.

1987    Suriname adopts a new constitution giving power to civilian leaders.

1989    The government and the Jungle Commando sign the Kourou Accord. Bouterse, still in
        charge of the military, refuses to honor the treaty.

1990    Bouterse overthrows President Ramsewak Shankar by telephone.

1991    Under international pressure, Suriname elects new civilian leaders. Ronald Venetiaan
        becomes president.

1992    The government and rebels reach a formal truce.

1993    Bouterse steps down from the military.

1996    The National Assembly elects Jules Wijdenbosch president of Suriname.

1999    Thousands demonstrate in Paramaribo against unemployment and inflation.

2000    Venetiaan is elected president again.

2004    Suriname and Guyana's border tensions increase when Suriname sends gunboats
        to force out an offshore oil company hired by Guyana.

2005    Venetiaan begins his third presidential term.

2007    The United Nations resolves a dispute between Guyana and Suriname over
        their territorial waters.

2008    The trial of Dési Bouterse for his role in the 1982 Fort Zeelandia execu-
        tions begins.

2009    Teachers, police, and other public employees stage a strike to pro-
        test a cut in their wages.

**COUNTRY NAME** Republic of Suriname

**AREA** 63,039 square miles (163,270 square km)

**MAIN LANDFORMS** coastal plain, northern savanna, highlands, Sipaliwini Savanna, Bakhuis Mountains, Wilhelmina Mountains, Van Asch van Wijk Mountains, Tumuc-Humac Mountains

**HIGHEST POINT** Juliana Top, 4,035 feet (1,230 m)

**LOWEST POINT** unnamed location in the coastal plain, 7 feet (2 m) below sea level

**MAJOR RIVERS** Coppename River, Corantijn River, Kabalebo River, Marowijne River, Nickerie River, Saramacca River, Suriname River, Tapanahoni River

**ANIMALS** anacondas, boa constrictors, bushmasters, caimans, capybaras, cocks-of-the-rock, dolphins, egrets, giant river otters, howler monkeys, jaguars, macaws, manatees, mata mata turtles, ocelots, parrots, poison dart frogs, pumas, scarlet ibises, sea otters, sea turtles, storks, tapirs, toucans, white herons

**CAPITAL CITY** Paramaribo

**OTHER MAJOR CITIES** Lelydorp, Nieuw Nickerie

**OFFICIAL LANGUAGE** Dutch

**MONETARY UNIT** Surinamese dollar. 100 cents = 1 dollar.

## SURINAMESE CURRENCY

The currency of Suriname is the Surinamese dollar. Its international currency code is SRD, and its written symbol is $. The government introduced the Surinamese dollar in 2004 to replace the colonial Surinamese guilder. Paper notes come in denominations of 1, 2.5, 5, 10, 20, 50, and 100 dollars. Coins come in denominations of 1, 5, 10, 25, 100, and 250 cents.

Suriname adopted its flag on November 25, 1975, when the nation gained independence. The flag shows five horizontal bands of red, white, and green. In the center is a wide red band. A large five-pointed gold star lies in the middle of the red band. Above and below the red band are two narrow white bands. Flanking these are two slightly wider green bands. The star stands for unity, sacrifice, and a prosperous future. The red band symbolizes progress and love. The white bands represent peace, freedom, and justice. The green bands represent fertility and hope.

Johannes Corstianus de Puy wrote the music for Suriname's national anthem in 1876. Cornelis Atses Hoekstra wrote the Dutch words to the anthem in 1893. In 1959 Henry F. de Ziel wrote a second set of lyrics with a different meaning in Sranan Tongo. The official anthem includes both sets of lyrics, but the Surinamese usually sing only the Sranan ones. The Sranan lyrics and their English translation appear below. To see the musical notation, hear the melody, and read the Dutch lyrics, visit http://www.nationalanthems.info/sr.htm.

### Opo Kondreman Oen Opo!

Opo kondreman oen opo!
Sranan gron e kari oen.
Wans ope tata komopo,
Wi moes seti kondre boen.
Stre de f'stre wi no sa frede.
Gado de wi fesi man.
Heri libi te na dede,
Wi sa feti gi Sranan.

### Rise, Countrymen, Rise!

Rise, countrymen, rise!
The soil of Suriname is calling you.
Wherever our ancestors came from,
We should take care of our country.
We are not afraid to fight.
God is our leader.
Our whole life until our death,
We will fight for Suriname.

For a link to a site where you can listen to Suriname's national anthem, "Opo Kondreman Oen Opo!", visit www.vgsbooks.com.

**HENCK ARRON** (1936–2000) Born in Paramaribo, Arron was the prime minister of Suriname from 1973 to 1980. He led Suriname to independence by forming alliances among Suriname's ethnic groups and political parties. He lost his position in the 1980 military coup led by Dési Bouterse.

**DÉSI BOUTERSE** (b. 1945) Bouterse led the military overthrow of Suriname's civilian government in 1980. He was born in the town of Dornburg. He led the nation until 1988. Many Surinamese hold him responsible for the 1982 murders of opponents of his regime. The Netherlands has issued a warrant for his arrest for drug trafficking, but he remains an active political leader in Suriname.

**RONNIE BRUNSWIJK** (b. ca. 1962) Brunswijk led a rural revolt against the military government of Suriname in the late 1980s and early 1990s. He formed the Jungle Commando militia after losing his post as Bouterse's bodyguard. He ordered many acts of economic sabotage (for example, on bauxite mines and hydroelectric plants) against the harsh regime. When civilian government returned, Brunswijk became a politician. In 2005 he won election to the National Assembly.

**RAMDEW CHAITOE** (1942–1994) Surinamese musician Chaitoe took inspiration from the rhythms and melodies of the Caribbean and India. Born in rural Suriname, he learned how to play the harmonium (a type of organ) from his father, an expert musician. He became a popular singer in a genre called chutney.

**EDGAR DAVIDS** (b. 1973) This famous soccer player was born in Paramaribo. Like many Surinamese, Davids played the game from a very young age. He became a professional in 1991. He has played for many of the best squads in Europe, including Milan and Juventus in Italy and Barcelona in Spain.

**ANTON DE KOM** (1898–1945) De Kom was a Creole leader born in Paramaribo. He led a movement during the 1930s demanding an end to Dutch colonial rule. Arrested and exiled to the Netherlands, he wrote *We Slaves of Suriname* there to describe the experiences of people living under a colonial government. He fought in the Dutch resistance against the Germans during World War II. He died in a German prison camp.

**ERWIN DE VRIES** (b. 1929) A renowned sculptor, de Vries was born in Paramaribo. He has lived in Suriname and the Netherlands. He studied in Europe and took part in group shows with Pablo Picasso and other famous artists. He designed a monument in Amsterdam, commemorating the colonial slave trade.

**ILONKA ELMONT** (b. 1974) A kickboxing champion who lives in the Netherlands, Elmont was born in Paramaribo. She is known around the world as the "Killer Queen." She began training in 1999. Since then she has won the women's world title in *muay thai* (Thai kickboxing) three times. She has also begun training for mixed martial arts bouts.

**JOHAN FERRIER** (b. 1910) Ferrier was the last governor of Dutch Guiana before it became Suriname. Then he became the first president of independent Suriname. He was born in Paramaribo. Dési Bouterse overthrew Ferrier in 1980. Ferrier moved to the Netherlands. He eventually wrote a book of children's stories, *The Big Anansi Book*.

**CYNTHIA MCLEOD** (b. 1936) A novelist born in Paramaribo, McLeod specializes in historic settings and characters. Her father was Johan Ferrier. She became a high school teacher after studying in the Netherlands. She traveled with her husband, a Surinamese ambassador, to Belgium and the United States. In 1987 she published her first novel, *The High Price of Sugar*, which became a best seller. She has since published several more historical novels set on Suriname's colonial plantations.

**ANTHONY NESTY** (b. 1967) Nesty is an elite swimmer specializing in the butterfly stroke. He was born in Trinidad and moved to Suriname as a young boy. He competed at the 1984 Summer Olympics in Los Angeles, California. In the late 1980s and early 1990s, he won medals in several international competitions. These included a gold in the 1988 Seoul Olympics and a bronze in the 1992 Barcelona Olympics. Nesty was the second black athlete ever to win an Olympic swimming medal. Suriname honored this feat by illustrating a banknote with an athlete swimming the butterfly. Nesty is a swimming coach at the University of Florida.

**ROBIN RAVALES** (1935–1983) Also known by his nickname Dobru, Ravales is considered Suriname's national poet. Born in Paramaribo, he wrote poetry in Sranan Tongo, the common tongue of Suriname. He was active politically, helping to found the National Republican Party. His most famous poem is "Wan Bon" ("One Tree"), which describes the mix of cultures in Suriname.

**JOHN GABRIEL STEDMAN** (1744–1797) A military officer, Stedman was born in the Netherlands. He sailed to Dutch Guiana in 1772 to fight against rebellious Maroons in the countryside. Stedman wrote about his experience in *Narrative of a Five Years' Expedition against the Revolted Negroes of Surinam*. This book is the most important historical source on the Maroons and the slave population of colonial Dutch Guiana.

**BROWNSBERG NATURE PARK** This park lies on a plateau in the northern savanna, about 81 miles (130 km) south of Paramaribo. Brownsberg teems with wildlife and offers a magnificent view over W. J. van Blommestein Lake.

**CENTRAL SURINAME NATURE RESERVE** This huge area of protected tropical rain forest covers 4 million acres (1.6 million hectares). It links the Raleigh Vallen, Tafelberg, and Eilerts de Haangebergte Nature Reserves. It includes Raleigh Vallen rapids; Foengoe Island, which is world famous among bird-watchers; and the Tafel Berg tepui. It shelters many endangered species, including jaguars, harpy eagles, giant armadillos, and scarlet macaws.

**FORT ZEELANDIA** British settlers raised this fortress in the mid-1600s and named it Fort Willoughby. Soon afterward the Dutch captured and renamed it. The fort, located in central Paramaribo, houses the Suriname Museum. Modern Surinamese remember Fort Zeelandia as a notorious prison used to hold political prisoners during the 1980s.

**FREDERIKSDORP** Frederiksdorp is a restored colonial plantation on the Commewijne River. From the mid-1700s to the late 1800s, Frederiksdorp grew coffee for export. After that, it grew cacao trees. In addition to farming and living facilities, the plantation includes a hospital, police station, jail, and school.

**GALIBI NATURE RESERVE** This stretch of beach in northern Suriname is famous as a nesting site for several sea turtle species, including the olive ridley and the huge leatherback. The turtles struggle up the beach in the late spring and summer to lay their eggs. The reserve is also close to a pair of Carib villages.

**KASIKASIMA TOP** This series of twelve granite peaks lies in an isolated region of southern Suriname. Visitors reach the spot by a long river journey in dugout canoes and by hiking over jungle trails.

**PARAMARIBO** The capital of Suriname holds many interesting sights. At the heart of the city lies Independence Square, flanked by the Presidential Palace and the National Assembly building. In older neighborhoods, Dutch colonial homes line the streets. The city also offers visitors the chance to inspect Fort Zeelandia, the Cupchiik Coliseum, the Numismatic Museum, and Saints Peter and Paul Cathedral.

**W. J. VAN BLOMMESTEIN LAKE** This is a large artificial lake in northeast Suriname, formed by Afobaka Dam on the Suriname River. Tonka Island, on the edge of the lake, houses a bustling ecotourism lodge built by a Maroon community.

**animism:** a system of belief in spirits that inhabit natural places, beings, things, and the everyday world and that influence human lives and fortunes

**Boeroes:** modern Surinamese descendants of Dutch colonists

**colony:** a territory controlled by a foreign power

**constitution:** a document defining the basic principles and laws of a nation

**Creole:** a modern Surinamese person descended from Africans and Europeans

**deforestation:** the loss of forests due to logging or clearing land for human uses. Deforestation leads to soil erosion, loss of wildlife habitat, and global warming.

**democracy:** government by the people through free elections

**free-market economy:** an economic system in which individuals or private companies own most goods and means of production. In a free-market economy, private decisions and market competition determine investments, prices, and distribution of goods and earnings.

**garimpeiro:** Portuguese word for miner. In Suriname, *garimpeiro* refers to a self-employed, unlicensed gold miner—usually from Brazil—working along streams in the southern rain forest.

**Guiana:** European name for the northeastern coast of South America. The Guiana region includes modern Guyana, Suriname, and French Guiana.

**hydroelectricity:** electric power produced by damming a river and then harnessing the energy of rushing water at hydroelectric power stations

**inflation:** a persistent rise in prices

**Jungle Commando:** the informal army led by Ronnie Brunswijk against the military government of Suriname in the late 1980s and early 1990s. The Jungle Commando's formal name was the Suriname National Liberation Army.

**junta:** a group of people controlling a government, usually after seizing power by force from the previous government

**Maroons:** escaped slaves who built independent villages in the remote interior of Suriname, or their descendants, who continue to live much as their ancestors did

**nomad:** a person who moves from place to place in search of pasture and water for livestock or in search of better hunting grounds

**plantations:** large farms producing cash crops, such as sugarcane or rice

**polder:** a raised terrace of earth surrounded by a ditch to hold rainwater and prevent flooding

**Sranan Tongo:** Suriname tongue. Sranan Tongo is a language used throughout Suriname. It blends African languages, English, Portuguese, and Dutch.

**telephone coup:** the 1990 overthrow of Suriname's civilian government by military commander Dési Bouterse. Instead of staging an armed rebellion, Bouterse simply phoned Suriname's leaders and told them to resign.

Colchester, Marcus. *Forest Politics in Suriname.* Utrecht, the Netherlands: International Books, 1995.
The author describes how mining and logging operations in Suriname's rain forest disrupt rural communities and bring violent conflict.

Dew, Edward M. *The Trouble in Suriname, 1975–1993.* Westport, CT: Praeger, 1994.
The author describes the political and economic turmoil experienced by Suriname from its independence in 1975 to the end of military rule.

Gordon, Raymond G. *Ethnologue: Languages of the World.* 15th ed. Dallas: SIL International, 2005.
This book is a window on Suriname's diverse ethnic groups. It provides detailed descriptions of the languages and dialects spoken in Suriname, including locations, alternate names, classifications, and maps. It also directs readers to many other publications, such as dictionaries and scholarly articles, that discuss Surinamese languages and cultures.

Hoogbergen, Wim. *The Boni Maroon Wars in Surname.* Aylesbury, United Kingdom: Brill Books, 1990.
This book describes a community of escaped slaves who settled near the French Guiana border and posed a constant threat to Dutch Guiana's colonists.

Kambel, Ellen-Rose, and Fergus MacKay. *The Rights of Indigenous Peoples and Maroons in Suriname.* Copenhagen, Denmark: International Work Group for Indigenous Affairs, 1999.
This book details the legal and political conflicts among European settlers, African slaves, and indigenous groups in colonial Suriname. The book also covers the constitution of 1987 and the debate over preservation and ownership of natural resources.

Plotkin, Mark J. *Tales of a Shaman's Apprentice: An Ethnobotanist Searches for New Medicines in the Amazon Rain Forest.* Gloucester, MA: Peter Smith Publishers, 2001.
The author treks through the rain forests of Suriname and Brazil to find useful plants unknown to medical science. He learns a great deal from indigenous shamans and warns against the destruction of the forest and the loss of valuable species.

*Population Reference Bureau.* March 26, 2009.
http://www.prb.org (April 3, 2009)
The bureau offers current population figures, vital statistics, land area, and more. Special articles cover the latest environmental and health issues that concern each country.

Price, Richard. *Maroon Societies: Rebel Slave Communities in the Americas.* Baltimore: Johns Hopkins University Press, 1996.
This history of escaped slaves and their independent communities covers the Caribbean, North America, and South America. The author includes many first-person and eyewitness accounts of Maroons and their experiences.

**Price, Richard, and Sally Price.** *Two Evenings in Saramaka.* Chicago: University of Chicago Press, 1991.
The author weaves legends and tales from the Saramaccan Maroon community. These stories explain the history of the world and human society. Magical occurrences are commonplace.

*The World Factbook.* **April 2, 2009.**
https://www.cia.gov/library/publications/the-world-factbook/geos/ns.html (April 3, 2009)
This website features up-to-date information about the people, land, economy, and government of Suriname. It also briefly covers transnational issues.

### The Amerindians of Suriname
http://www.centrelink.org/Suriname.html

This page provides dozens of updated links to articles on indigenous peoples and their culture, as well as Surinamese history, archaeology, and environmental conservation.

### BBC News Country Profile: Suriname
http://news.bbc.co.uk/2/hi/americas/country_profiles/1211306.stm

This helpful site provides a quick overview of Suriname's recent history, political events, and economic development.

### Lonely Planet Suriname
http://www.lonelyplanet.com/the-guianas/suriname

This website offers a useful and easy-to-navigate travel guide to Suriname. It includes pages on history, getting around the country, work and study, practical information, and maps. The editors also choose five "top pick" destinations and provide information on Kasikasima Top.

**Price, Sally, and Richard Price. *Maroon Arts: Cultural Vitality in the African Diaspora*. Boston: Beacon Press, 1999.**

This book studies the colorful and vibrant artwork of Maroon communities in modern Suriname and several other regions of the Caribbean basin.

### ReadyTex Art Gallery
http://www.readytexartgallery.com

Visitors to this website can view dozens of works by Surinamese artists and craftspeople, including several mentioned in this book. The site also provides artist biographies.

**Rogonzinski, Jan. *A Brief History of the Caribbean: From the Arawak and Carib to the Present*. New York: Plume, 2000.**

This volume offers a detailed history of the entire Caribbean basin, from the first voyage of Christopher Columbus to the present day.

**Sirvaitis, Karen. *Guyana in Pictures*. Minneapolis: Twenty-First Century Books, 2010.**

This book examines Guyana's history, society, and culture, including its interactions with Suriname.

**Szulc-Krzyzanowski, Michel, and Michiel van Kempen. *Deep-Rooted Words: Ten Storytellers and Writers from Surinam (South America)*. Amsterdam, the Netherlands: Uitgeverij Voetnoot, 1992.**

This book provides an interesting survey of modern Surinamese writers, showing how their works draw on storytelling traditions of the country's various ethnic groups.

### UNICEF: Suriname
http://www.unicef.org/infobycountry/suriname_statistics.html

This website of the United Nations Children's Fund provides news updates, real-life stories, and statistics on population, health, education, and other issues affecting the lives of children in Suriname.

**Further Reading and Websites**

### U.S. Department of State Background Note: Suriname
http://www.state.gov/r/pa/ei/bgn/1893.htm

This U.S. Department of State site provides information useful for visitors. In addition to practical knowledge such as visa requirements, current health issues, political conditions, and travel warnings, the site also offers basic information on Suriname's people, history, government, and economy.

### vgsbooks.com
http://www.vgsbooks.com

Visit vgsbooks.com, the homepage of the Visual Geography Series®. You can get linked to all sorts of useful online information, including geographical, historical, demographic, cultural, and economic websites. The vgsbooks.com site is a great resource for late-breaking news and statistics.

### Welsbacher, Anne. *Protecting Earth's Rain Forests*. Minneapolis: Lerner Publications Company, 2009.

Rain forests house important natural resources for Suriname and countries worldwide. Learn more about rain forests and the necessity of preserving them.

### Williams, Colleen Madonna Flood. *Suriname*. Broomall, PA: Mason Crest, 2003.

This book introduces middle-grade readers to Suriname, with information on the country's geography, history, economy, and culture.

**Captions for photos appearing on cover and chapter openers:**

Cover: Blue poison dart frogs live in the forests of southern Suriname.

pp. 4–5 Densely forested land surrounds W. J. van Blommestein Lake in northeastern Suriname.

pp. 8–9 A waterfall feeds a small pool in the Central Suriname Nature Reserve.

pp. 18–19 Ancient rock carvings appear at a site called Werehpai in southern Suriname.

pp. 36–37 A group of Indian Surinamese farmers rests during the rice harvest.

pp. 44–45 A woman prays with a Hindu priest at a temple in Paramaribo.

pp. 56–57 Employees of Staatsolie, the national oil company, work at an oil well in Suriname.

**Photo Acknowledgments**

The images in this book are used with the permission of: : © Frans Lemmens/ The Image Bank/Getty Images, pp. 4–5, 16, 18–19, 44–45; © XNR Productions, pp. 6, 10; © Robert Caputo/Aurora/Getty Images, pp. 8–9, 36–37, 38, 49; © LITTLEHALES, BATES/Animals Animals, p. 13; © Ron Giling/Peter Arnold, Inc., pp. 15, 39, 48, 56–57, 61, 64; The Granger Collection, New York, p. 21; Private Collection/The Bridgeman Art Library, p. 22; Bibliotheque Nationale, Paris, France/Archives Charmet/The Bridgeman Art Library, p. 24; © Frans Lemmens/Alamy, pp. 27, 40, 58, 60; © Bettmann/CORBIS, pp. 28, 29; © Claude Urraca/Sygma/CORBIS, p. 30; © Patrick Chauvel/Sygma/CORBIS, p. 31; AP Photo/Edward Troon, p. 33; © Thomas Coex/AFP/Getty Images, p. 34; © Picture Contact/Alamy, pp. 41, 50, 54, 63; © Jan Baks/Alamy, p. 43; REUTERS/Ranu Abhelakh, pp. 46, 52; © Ertugrul Kilic, p. 47; © Bob Thomas/ Bob Thomas Sports Photography/Getty Images, p. 51; © Jason Rothe/Alamy, p. 53; Image courtesy of Banknotes.com - Audrius Tomonis, p. 68; © Laura Westlund/Independent Picture Service, p. 69.

Front Cover: © Gail Shumway/Taxi/Getty Images. Back Cover: NASA.